THE SELF AND PERSONALITY STRUCTURE

Core concepts in therapy

Series editor: Michael Jacobs

Over the last ten years a significant shift has taken place in the relations between representatives of different schools of therapy. Instead of the competitive and often hostile reactions we once expected from each other, therapists from different points of the spectrum of approaches are much more interested in where they overlap and where they differ. There is a new sense of openness to cross orientation learning.

The Core Concepts in Therapy series compares and contrasts the use of similar terms across a range of the therapeutic models, and seeks to identify where different terms appear to denote similar concepts. Each book is authored by two therapists, each one from a distinctly different orientation; and where possible each one from a different continent, so that an international dimension becomes a feature of this network of ideas.

Each of these short volumes examines a key concept in psychological therapy, setting out comparative positions in a spirit of free and critical enquiry, but without the need to prove one model superior to another. The books are fully referenced and point beyond themselves to the wider literature on each topic.

Forthcoming and published titles:

THE SELF AND PERSONALITY STRUCTURE

Paul Brinich
and
Christopher Shelley

Open University Press
Buckingham • Philadelphia

Open University Press
Celtic Court
22 Ballmoor
Buckingham
MK18 1XW

email: enquiries@openup.co.uk
world wide web: www.openup.co.uk

and
325 Chestnut Street
Philadelphia, PA 19106, USA

First Published 2002

A catalogue record of this book is available from the British Library

ISBN 0 335 20564 X (hb)   0 335 20563 1 (pb)

Library of Congress Cataloging-in-Publication Data
Brinich, Paul M., 1946–
   The self and personality structure / Paul Brinich and
   Christopher Shelley.
      p. cm. – (Core concepts in therapy)
   Includes bibliographical references (p.) and index.
   ISBN 0-335-20564-X – ISBN 0-335-20563-1 (pbk.)
   1. Self. 2. Psychotherapy. I. Shelley, Christopher.
   II. Title. III. Series.
RC489.S43 B75 2002
616.89′14–dc21   2001056025

Typeset by Graphicraft Limited, Hong Kong
Printed in Great Britain by The Cromwell Press, Trowbridge

Contents

Series editor's preface

A major aspect of intellectual and cultural life in the twentieth century has been the study of psychology – present of course for many centuries in practical form and expression in the wisdom and insight to be found in spirituality, in literature and in the dramatic arts, as well as in arts of healing and guidance, both in the East and West. In parallel with the deepening interest in the inner processes of character and relationships in the novel and theatre in the nineteenth century, psychiatry reformulated its understanding of the human mind, and encouraged, in those brave enough to challenge the myths of mental illness, new methods of exploration of psychological processes.

The twentieth century witnessed, especially in its latter half, an explosion of interest both in theories about personality, psychological development, cognition and behaviour, as well as in the practice of therapy, or perhaps more accurately, the therapies. It also saw, as is not uncommon in any intellectual discipline, battles between theories and therapists of different persuasions, particularly between psychoanalysis and behavioural psychology, and each in turn with humanistic and transpersonal therapies, and also within the major schools themselves. If such arguments are not surprising, and indeed objectively can be seen as healthy – potentially promoting greater precision in research, alternative approaches to apparently intractable problems, and deeper understanding of the wellsprings of human thought, emotion and behaviour – it is nonetheless disturbing that for many decades there was such a degree of sniping and entrenchment of positions from therapists who should have been able to look more closely at their own responses and rivalries. It is as if diplomats had ignored their skills and knowledge and resorted in their dealings with each other to gun slinging.

The psychotherapeutic enterprise has also been an international one. There were a large number of centres of innovation, even at the beginning – Paris, Moscow, Vienna, Berlin, Zurich, London, Boston USA; and soon Edinburgh, Rome, New York, Chicago and California saw the development of different theories and therapeutic practice. Geographical location has added to the richness of the discipline, particularly identifying cultural and social differences, and widening the psychological debate to include, at least in some instances, socio-logical and political dimensions.

The question has to be asked, given the separate developments due to location, research interests, personal differences, and splits between and within traditions, whether what has sometimes been called 'psycho-babble' is indeed a welter of different languages describing the same phenomena through the particular jargon and theorizing of the various psychotherapeutic schools. Or are there genuine differences, which may lead sometimes to the conclusion that one school has got it right, while another has therefore got it wrong; or that there are 'horses for courses'; or, according to the Dodo principle, that 'all shall have prizes'?

The latter part of the twentieth century saw some rapproche-ment between the different approaches to the theory and practice of psychotherapy (and counselling), often due to the external pressures towards organizing the profession responsibly and to the high stand-ards demanded of it by health care, by the public and by the state. It is out of this budding rapprochement that there came the motiva-tion for this series, in which a number of key concepts that lie at the heart of the psychotherapies can be compared and contrasted across the board. Some of the terms used in different traditions may prove to represent identical concepts; others may look similar, but in fact highlight quite different emphases, which may or may not prove useful to those who practise from a different perspective; other terms, apparently identical, may prove to mean something completely dif-ferent in two or more schools of psychotherapy.

In order to carry out this project it seemed essential that as many of the psychotherapeutic traditions as possible should be represented in the authorship of the series; and to promote both this, and the spirit of dialogue between traditions, it seemed also desirable that there should be two authors for each book, each one representing, where practicable, different orientations. It was important that the series should be truly international in its approach and therefore in its authorship; and that miracle of late twentieth-century technology, the Internet, proved to be a productive means of finding authors, as well as a remarkably efficient method of communicating, in the cases of some pairs of authors, halfway across the world.

This series therefore represents, in a new millennium, an extremely exciting development, one which as series editor I have found more and more enthralling as I have eavesdropped on the drafts shuttling back and forth between authors. Here, for the first time, the reader will find all the major concepts of all the principal schools of psychotherapy and counselling (and not a few minor ones) drawn together so that they may be compared, contrasted, and (it is my hope) above all used – used for the ongoing debate between orientations, but more importantly still, used for the benefit of clients and patients who are not at all interested in partisan positions, but in what works, or in what throws light upon their search for healing and understanding.

Michael Jacobs

Preface

For the purpose of this series, we ask: what difference does the *self* make for the theory and practice of counselling and psychotherapy? The self – itself – seems to be an obvious and integral feature of professional work in these fields. Indeed, is not the self de facto what the person brings to the therapy room? If so, is it not therefore a fundamental feature of the mental health professions? Some may be surprised that there isn't consensus on this issue. It appears, however, that most therapy and personality school modalities both accept and make use of the self within their diverse approaches. This volume explores the theoretical issues that intersect both the self and personality. Two other volumes in this series are directly related to this one. *The Therapist's Use of Self* (Rowan and Jacobs) considers applied issues, while *Character and Personality Types* (Totton and Jacobs) considers various approaches to personality and character typology.

In psychology the self has emerged only slowly. This is despite the fact that the birth of psychology as a discipline in the late nineteenth century, best exemplified in the work of William James, included an elaborate analysis of the self. His celebrated analysis constitutes an early apex of the self. Its glory was short lived and its decline followed. Derided as hopelessly subjectivistic, frowned on and tainted as capricious, psychology generally cast the self aside. Late nineteenth-century conceptions of good science required strict discipline and control, both of which the evasive self, saturated in Romanticism, defied. Therefore its expulsion ensued and suddenly the self was nowhere to be seen. In academic psychology it had all but disappeared. In the associated and emerging schools of psychotherapy, the self was explicitly absent (though perhaps assumed to exist) as it was in classical psychoanalysis; or expunged and erased, as it was in behaviourism. Those schools that embraced the self occupied marginal positions, bucking the trend of strict, functional objectivism. Indeed, behaviourists denied that such things as selves, minds and, in some cases, even consciousness existed. Those behaviourists who acknowledged consciousness disavowed its significance without considering consciousness as the light of the self. The function of action and conduct overshadowed all other considerations. These views had a tremendous effect on twentieth-century psychology and its applied disciplines.

It was in direct reaction to dominant behaviourism and other corners of positivistic psychology and psychiatry that dissenting schools surfaced. Under the humanistic and existential umbrellas *third force* psychology, which gained prominence during the 1960s, challenged the variable and anti-self models so widely accepted in academic, hence for the period, behavioural and experimental psychology. The third force argued that this overemphasis on objective behaviour distorted the human subject by denying phenomenology, a perspective the self had always contained.

While third force psychology did not come to dominate, it did encourage the development of new subdisciplines particularly the expansion and proliferation of counselling psychology. In many universities, counselling psychology departments developed separately from academic psychology and psychiatry, often in departments of education. Other champions of the phenomenal self, which third force psychology extols, emerged through traditions such as social work, pastoral counselling, guidance movements, and so on. The cross-fertilization that these traditions brought into third force psychology profoundly affected the manner in which professional services were offered. Hitherto, most psychotherapy or analysis had been conducted by medical doctors, the exception being behaviour therapy. The third force, however, included practitioners who, with few exceptions, came to the work of therapy without backgrounds in medicine. The nature of mental health delivery was changing and the re-emergence of the self was intertwined with these changes.

During the 1960s the self came back in vogue. Then as now everyone wanted a take on this intimate friend. Encounter groups and *self*-help trends emerged and flourished where many began a journey of self-discovery. Today it would appear that most non-medical models of therapy subscribe to some theoretical notion of self. It therefore seems sensible to deconstruct and make as transparent as possible what is meant by *self*. This is where theories of personality come into play for it is personality theories that generally seek to describe the enduring developmental uniqueness of self.

In this book we outline the concept of the self as represented in several domains of personality theory. In so doing, we explore the self as it appears in some of the more central schools of psychotherapy. To begin this journey, we turn back and try to understand something about the idea of self as it has been represented throughout western history. In this regard, we are recognizing that *self* is a very old concept whereas counselling and psychotherapy, in the greater scheme of things, are rather new innovations. By viewing the self as subject to historical production, we answer our critics who have argued that the psychological disciplines generally fail to take into account historical situatedness and therefore social context (Tolman 1994). However, as brief as this selection of historical representation is, it is limited in other ways. The western view of self necessarily truncates and limits analysis as it excludes philosophical understandings of the self from eastern and aboriginal discourses, discourses that hold a very rich and copious series of narrative and written accounts on the self topic (Tu 1985). A vast concept such as self can never be fully explicated in a book such as this. We hope, however, to whet the readers' appetite and encourage greater interest in a frequently taken-for-granted notion.

Pluralism in the psychological disciplines

As counsellors, therapists and so forth, what value is there to presenting a collection of perspectives on personality and the self? Monte suggests that

> the history of personality theory exposes human nature reflecting on it*self*. It is a psychohistory, illuminated by the human character of its creators and opaqued by the character of their human limits.
>
> (Monte 1987: 9, our italics)

The act of reflecting on the self and associated notions such as personality creates a conundrum of sorts. Jung wrote: 'never forget that in psychology the *means* by which you judge and observe the psyche is the *psyche* itself. Have you ever heard of a hammer beating itself? In psychology the observer is the observed' (1968: 141–2, our italics). Foucault (1965) also recognized psychology's central epistemological problem, that of the observer being embedded in the observed.

Though grounded in various standpoints, theorists of personality generally grapple with the problem of human subjectivity. In academic psychology, personality measures attempt to objectively describe endurable aspects of our selves in all its subjective wonder. Other theorists use inductivism and case studies to produce general theories of personality inclusive of any associated psychopathology. There are an overwhelming number of such theories and associated schools. For example, Corsini (1981) has identified 250 different schools of psychotherapy. Therefore, to take a pluralistic approach to the self and personality seems apposite for a volume such as this.

Samuels outlines the benefits of viewing the psyche as plural. By extension, he views a pluralist as 'one who knows that he or she does not know everything and is prepared to listen to a more informed source' (1989: 7). In this scope, Samuels also notes that there remains an 'antipluralist tenor' in many aspects of contemporary psychological discourse. The realm of the human self is fraught with controversy and perhaps this is what makes the topic so invigorating and pregnant with interest.

Our take on the self in the psychological disciplines is not unbiased. Paul (Brinich) is a child psychoanalyst grounded in Anna Freud's tradition; Chris (Shelley) is a psychotherapist in the Adlerian tradition. We both have our feet firmly rooted in specific (and limited) perspectives. Writing this book has broadened our understandings and given us an opportunity to appreciate the diversity in the field.

By adopting a pluralistic tenor, we had to put ourselves to school, so to speak, and find out what we could about other major contributions to the self and personality. We divided our labour accordingly: Paul wrote chapters 2, 3 and 4; Chris wrote chapters 1, 5, 6, 7 and 8. Each of us acted as editors and critics to the other's work. And while the chapters were written fairly independently, each of us are in this regard present in all of the chapters.

In reflecting back on the project, we found that it was an interesting exercise. To the best of our knowledge, it is the first time a psychoanalyst and an Adlerian have collaborated on a book together. The tendency set by such a pairing is to explore and appreciate differences. The differences that exist in the self and personality fields are copious. We were challenged by the sheer weight of the topics, the self especially is dense and complex, to which many an erudite scholar have spent perhaps a lifetime contemplating. On the other hand, personality as an area of study has produced enough data to fill scores of library shelves. To fairly summarize even a portion of this data is ambitious indeed. It was nevertheless a satisfying journey into exploring these discourses and representing our selections in this volume. We certainly learned from delving into the many approaches that the self and personality have to offer.

The book idea as part of the Core Concepts in Therapy series was conceived while Chris was still resident in the UK. The collaboration with Paul in the United States made the partnership international. With such physical distances between us, the wonders of the internet became a necessary tool. In the early stages of writing Chris took the opportunity to move back to his native Canada and now practises out of Vancouver. Our chapters bounced back and forth from Canada, to the United States, and to England (for Michael's input and suggestions) before bouncing back to North America. If there was a cyberspace air miles scheme we would all be off on several holidays!

Acknowledgements

Paul: Writing about perspectives other than one's own is a challenge and I must thank Michael Jacobs, the editor of this series, for issuing that challenge. I am also grateful for the gentle but persistent prodding that my co-author, Christopher Shelley, provided as this project sometimes fell victim to the many other priorities with which it had to compete. Further thanks go to my colleagues at the Children's Psychiatric Institute of John Umstead Hospital and in the Department of Psychology at the University of North Carolina at Chapel Hill.

Chris: The editorial assistance we received from Professor Valerie Raoul, The University of British Columbia, and Dr Emmy Van Deurzen of the Psychotherapy Section, British Psychological Society was invaluable. The series editor, Michael Jacobs was enormously supportive and I thank him for all of his patient assistance. I am also grateful for the continued support I receive from afar from my British Adlerian colleagues. Thanks also to Susan Cosco in Toronto. The friendships I continue to experience with so many in my community in east Vancouver sustained and nurtured me through this project. Thanks to: Shelly Fahey, Anton Pillipa, Robert Haley and Roddy Macdonald for their enduring support.

CHAPTER 1

The self and personality in context

[the self is] the most puzzling puzzle with which psychology has to deal
(William James)

Forming questions about the *self* and the corollary notion of *personality* is a challenge. First, the self is a topic of interest to many disciplines, but this multidisciplinarity renders the concept all the more complex. Adding the issue of personality to an understanding of the self deepens the complexity, even though it was a conjunction of these two concepts that was integral to the birth of the psychotherapies. Indeed, most of the great founding therapists and counsellors have also been personality theorists of one variety or another. Consequently, this book concerns itself with the way different theories of counselling and psychotherapy view selfhood within a context of personhood. Of these theories we ask, what makes the expression of one self unique and different from the expression of another?

This chapter aims to contextualize the self and personality so as to help us frame what it is that various schools of therapy say about each other. This requires that we go beyond the psychotherapies and into the depths of history, because much of what the psychological disciplines say about the self and personality originates in philosophy and religion. What specific religious traditions have to say about the matter is beyond our current brief, although there is significant overlap between some philosophical and religious discourses on the self. Indeed, one discovers that the self overlaps and intersects with many deeply studied and relevant realms. Creating some background understanding of the self and personality therefore seems appropriate, since they constellate so many complex questions for contemplation.

The self in western history

An historical perspective suggests that what the self was in yester-years is not necessarily what 'it' is today. The Zeitgeist, that is the spirit of an age, affects the development of such concepts in profound ways. A sketch of the self through western history will help to organize understanding and intersection.

It is useful to recall that, in the western world, the notion of the self has perplexed scholars of all varieties since antiquity. Greek philosophical writings put forward the Socratic instruction to *know thyself*; this obviously begs the question, what *is* the 'self'? Plato (429–347 BC) also outlined the 'care for the self' as stated in his *Alcibiades*. Later, Christianity promoted alternative views that diminished the individual self as a unit of importance and focused instead on the 'soul'. Christianity, like many other religious stances, privileges the notion of soul over self. Christian views on the soul would have a considerable impact on how the individual is understood. The scholastic philosophers (for example, Aquinas), who were the dominant western intellectual forces of the medieval era, generated views that predominated into the Renaissance. During the Renaissance there was a shift towards *humanism*, which placed human beings rather than God at the centre of the universe. This shift had important consequences for how the self was viewed during the age of reason (or Enlightenment) in the seventeenth and eighteenth centuries. This period would come to emphasize the significance of the individual, a person's rights, freedoms and responsibilities (liberalism).

Regardless of the particular historical emphasis, the self has remained an important construct in western thought for more than two millennia. Throughout this time the self's purported essence has been disputed on every imaginable ground. For some it is a necessary construct that makes individuals in all their uniqueness both coherent and knowable. For others it is merely a distraction from the immaterial soul or spirit. And for yet others the self does not exist at all but is merely an effect or contrivance of language.

In the process of exploring various theories of self and personality, we will discover that there is no single definition that can satisfy our current quest. This plurality is nothing new insofar as the self has always been a great intellectual and theoretical puzzle. Smuts understood this in his proclamation that the self constitutes: 'the great mystery, the most elusive phantom in the whole range of knowledge' (1973: 263). Seventy years following Smuts's declaration we find ourselves still grasping for this elusive phantom. Barglow points to the idea we have in the west, of possessing an internal self, as 'essential to our humanity' although it remains simultaneously intangible, 'this subjective centre or core . . . eludes our conceptual grasp' (1994: 3). Is it possible that the further we move into the future, the less concrete, fixed and solid the self becomes? Indeed, much contemporary theorizing on the concept puts this matter into question. Perhaps alarming to some, there are those who are now declaring the death of the self just as Nietzsche declared the death of God more than a century ago. Associated concepts such as identity, subjectivity and individuality are similarly disputed by many contemporary thinkers who have placed these concepts under 'discursive interrogation', that is a rereading against the grain (for example, Butler 1990b).

In order to understand how current discourse around the self in the psychotherapies has developed, it is important to view the concept as it has evolved over the past several centuries. For example, Shakespeare's noted words on the self have endured for a very long time and point to some assumptions worth analysing:

> This above all – to thine own self be true,
> And it must follow, as the night the day,
> Thou canst not then be false to any man.
>
> (*Hamlet*, I. iii. 75)

Shakespeare wrote about the self as a unified entity that one could *know* and therefore be true to. In Shakespeare we see the dawn of a self that is both independently capable and potentially separate from political, social and religious functions, a view that was rather radical for its period. However, during this transition into the Enlightenment period many were not fully in possession of individuated selves and were denied autonomous subjectivity; as MacCary (1998) points out, their feudal subjectivity was still subject to Elizabeth.

The 'self' of which Shakespeare spoke continued to be the object of suspicion and outright degradations. In France, Pascal (1623–62) proclaimed that: 'The self is hateful' (*Pensées*, no. 455). Grotstein (1999) also alludes to the pre-Enlightenment world-view that sustained a vitriolic characterization of self. Drawing on Jung, he notes that the alchemists of the Middle Ages postulated that men were made up of *homunculi*, an assortment of tiny gods and demons. Indeed, the predominant views of the pre-Enlightenment West held that the individual self was subject to intrusion by devilish forces, or at the mercy of other deterministic and external dynamics. For example, explanations for madness in Elizabethan times were based on a widespread belief in external rather than internal forces. MacCary summarizes the world-view of this period:

> Their religious beliefs allowed [Elizabethans] to seek specific traumatic experience; their astrology made planetary movement a factor; their medicine led them to blame glandular secretions. All of these are relatively external factors; none suggests a purely internal cause or self-contained collapse.
>
> (MacCary 1998: 31)

The Elizabethan age, in which Shakespeare had been embedded, followed the Middle Ages where representations of the self were cast largely in immoral terms. After the Roman empire fell and the teachings of the Catholic Church were spread, new views of the self would be propagated. Jesus, the scriptures read, would instruct followers to 'deny self' (Luke 9: 23–4). Only the reverence of holy figures was worthy of focus: 'Not I, but Christ' (Galatians 2: 20). The sinful view of the self was set up by the medieval supremacy of Christian theology. This theology viewed the human self as the fleshy site of Original sin, which must be neither indulged nor encouraged. This turn against the self would, curiously, survive the individualism emphasized in the Enlightenment and beyond. Perhaps the current western fixation on self-esteem can be traced and rooted here. After all, if we are filled with sin, then we are to be appraised accordingly, the less sinful the greater our value. We are instructed not to indulge self but 'esteem others' (Philippians 2: 3). Calvinist doctrine espoused the supremacy of God and salvation by faith, but also emphasized the virtues of hard work and material reward. Through this *Protestant ethic*, the following contradiction would come to colour the notion of self: society became more focused on the privatized and individually accountable self, whilst decrying the sinfulness of the *selfish*. These views saturated the creation and evolution of the word *self*. Danziger (1997: 143) points out that in the English language this word surfaced around the year 1300. He quotes the earliest surviving reference: 'Oure awn self we sal deny, And folow oure lord god al-mighty'. In the fourteenth century it was the influence of the religious scholastics that prevailed. Even through later so-called rationalistic periods, such as the Enlightenment, and more recently the dominance of late modernity, these historical views have persisted.

Linguistically, the word self holds an interesting place as a concept representative of a person's lived convergence of cultural contents (language, customs, symbols and so on) with subjective, individual experience. For some, this is all that we are and sufficiently so. For others, a divine spark underpins it all. As revealed earlier, an historical analysis of the idea of the self shows it to have been polarized from the very start; the individual self as a manifestation of wickedness, or the object of salvation and potential goodness, so long as it was subjugated to the will of the Church and the State.

Prior to the Enlightenment, a focus on the carnal self was seen as a distraction from the need for salvation and the goal of purity of soul. The soul represented the pinnacle of being, a non-material entity that was considered unified and the ultimate object of spiritual reflection. It was within the soul that one found one's connection to God. This was cast as both natural and unquestionable, a metaphysical fact. The Enlightenment sowed the seeds for the end of the soul in most rational and empirical circles. For example, in much of academic psychology, talk of the soul is forbidden, a taboo that reflects the discipline's materialistic and scientific background. This background was set by the philosophical writings of John Locke (1632–1704), an architect of the age of Enlightenment. Locke's *Essay Concerning Human Understanding* emphasized that the self could be known only as an empirical entity; we are born like a sheet of 'white paper', empty and waiting for experience to fill us. Locke placed great emphasis on reason and cast doubt on previous religious and scholastic beliefs. Through Locke, the self (as a phenomenon that could be observed) became empirically respectable, whereas the soul was dismissed as an unobservable phenomenon. The separation of self and soul was clearly a product of the Enlightenment, cemented at the dawn of late modernity (late nineteenth century), a period which produced many ideas that continue to dominate our thinking today.

Nineteenth-century perspectives on the self

Gergen (1991) has pointed out that the two periods most relevant to our current understandings of self are nineteenth-century Romanticism and twentieth-century (late) modernity. He argues that both periods have produced a strongly individualistic understanding of the self, even though many of the values associated with these periods are otherwise contradictory and incompatible. While romantic notions of selfhood continue to shape our understanding, such views have been sharply challenged by twentieth-century modernity.

Though individualism flourished beyond the Enlightenment, many continued to view a focus on the self with disdain. In the romantic period that followed, the way out of such loathsomeness was through *selflessness*. Romanticism espoused an idealism under which the self was expected to strive for perfection and moral virtue. Many of these ideals were unattainable (though relentlessly pursued). Such was the breeding ground for deep contradictions within the self. For women especially, the selfless ideal would be stressed. In Victorian times (a high point of Romanticism) it was pure and noble to be selfless; and carnal and wicked to be selfish. Eventually such statements were exposed as the ideological foundations of oppression; suffrage movements and first-wave feminism followed. Many were influenced by Marx's *historical materialism*, which challenged metaphysical statements on the 'naturalness' of the self by re-locating the self within the socio-political rather than the biological sphere. Critical methods derived from German philosophy encouraged interpretation of underlying presuppositions, so that ideals such as selflessness would not mystify the effects of industrial capitalism in reinforcing prevalent individualism.

The Victorians understood the need for a concept of self that was less barren than a view of human nature based purely on a reduction of nerve cells embedded in grey matter. Indeed, the self was seen as necessary to conceptualize individuals in all their depth and profundity – the self as a cherished entity carrying the hidden promise of perfection, constituted by immaterial sacredness and potential moral purity. Gergen writes that:

> much of our contemporary vocabulary of the person, along with associated ways of life, finds its origins in the romantic period. It is a vocabulary of passion, purpose, depth, and personal significance: a vocabulary that generates awe of heroes, of genius, and of inspired work.
>
> (Gergen 1991: 27)

The Victorians were well-informed about the deprivation and pain that characterized the lives of individual working-class people. Industrialization, widespread poverty, and public health problems due to increasing urbanization forced many people into squalid and desperate social conditions. Diseases such as consumption (tuberculosis) brought millions of people face-to-face with unbearable suffering.

The Romantic period was a somewhat anti-empirical time, things were presented as not what they appeared. It was clearly a period where many retreated into pre-Enlightenment sentiments. The clear, straightforward, surface empiricism enshrined in the Enlightenment was questioned. In preparing for the romantic period, Kant proclaimed: 'I have no knowledge of myself as I am but merely as I appear to myself. The consciousness of myself is thus very far from being a knowledge of the self' ([1781]1965: B. 158). The questioning of empiricism that Kant put forward amounted to a critique of the doctrine of justification and led into the philosophical currents of idealism from which philosophers such as Hegel took their lead. For example, Hegel put forward the following premise, summarized by Brod 'that what is familiar (*bekannt*) was often not really known (*erkannt*) precisely because it was so seemingly familiar' (Brod 1987: 2–3). Contemporary critical psychologists such as Tolman have extended this line of thinking by challenging the whole experimental project in psychology as based on 'naive empiricism' (1994: 24). This line of thinking polemically suggests that surface and abstracted observations of the self are bereft, the proverbial book caught in glaring judgement of its cover. However, the cessation of the empirical stance, if ever achieved, would be rather worrying. It may lead to mysticism and forms of superstition that hearken back to pre-Enlightenment superstition, dogmas and other slippery slopes. What the surface reveals is often the 'truth', and a useful one at that. That it is not necessarily the 'whole truth' is, we speculate, a sensible conclusion.

Popular culture in the nineteenth century suggests that in the deep interior, one could be possessed by demons resembling the mediaeval homunculi. Or, one could be a medium for the spirit of the deceased. Seances, which were popular in the Victorian years, invited the spirits of the dead to enter one's body, requesting the 'invasion' of one's self by an ethereal other for however short a period. In other folklore of the time it was suggested that perhaps one was not temporarily occupied by an invasive force of evil, perhaps one *was* already constituted by a dark and unknown side. Stevenson wrote of such a self divided in *The Strange Case of Dr. Jekyll and Mr. Hyde*,

> I thus drew steadily nearer to the truth, by whose partial discovery I have been doomed to such dreadful shipwreck: that man is not truly one, but truly two . . . and I hazard the guess that man will ultimately be known for a polity of multifarious, incongruous and independent denizens.
>
> (cited in Grotstein 1999: 28)

Twenty years following Stevenson's classic story, Prince (1906) documented the clinical phenomenon of multiple personality (now referred to as *dissociative identity disorder*). The instance of unknown alter-egos is not just a Victorian tale. Indeed, Ross (1999) has proposed a continuum of dissociation between the 'normal' multiplicity of the contemporary person (perhaps akin to Gergen's *saturated self*) and serious forms of dissociation as revealed in dissociative identity disorder.

In the nineteenth century, many were moved by romantic music, painting, literature, theatre and dance – and many moved away from the despair of the external world and into the dreamy deep interiority of the psyche. Escapism was certainly a theme of the times. Opium dens were common and so was absinthe. Hypnosis was popularized as a way of trying to understand the mysterious depths of the self. Strange ailments were cured by this method contributing to a new understanding of self affected by unconscious motivation. Out of this understanding psychoanalysis was born. This discourse developed towards the end of the period promising a scientific understanding of the deep self, the unknown wellspring, the producer of dreams. All of the Victorian closed-door, tight-laced, repressed sexuality spinning the passions would compel Freud to declare the largest and most powerful feature of the human psyche to be the *unconscious*.

Other romantic notions such as the striving for 'true' love through a conjunction of destined souls, also dominated the period. The assumption underlying these beliefs is that not only do we have a fixed essence that we may call self, but this self is destined to engage in preordained spiritual crossings. These fated interactions with others are the wellspring where 'true' love would emerge and a 'communion of souls' could take place (Gergen 1991: 227). This fatalistic view of self suggested that one was not ultimately in control of one's passions. Therefore, people in this period apparently compensated by adopting strategies of constraint and constriction, attempts to hide those wayward passions and confine them behind closed doors. The lessons drawn from this period would emphasize how impractical and frequently unattainable ideals of perfection, purity, morality and respectability were, no matter how desirable. This is the principle factor behind the emergence of twentieth-century modernity and its associated functionalism.

William James's legacy: between Romanticism and late modernity

It is arguable that no figure in the history of psychology has had a more thorough impact on our understanding of the self-concept than the pragmatist William James (1842–1910). Like Freud, Mead and Cooley, he occupied a unique position as a transitional figure between Romanticism and modernity. In his classic work, *The Principles of Psychology* (1890), James outlined his ideas on the self. The first distinction he made about the self was its divisible constitution between the 'me' and the 'I'. The 'me' is the publicly recognizable, objectively constituted, empirically knowable aspects of the self. The 'me' is constructed by the subjectively based agency James termed the 'I'. The 'me' self is the self as 'known' whereas the 'I' self is the self as 'knower'. This fundamental separation laid the groundwork for a modernist understanding of the self which, in academic psychology, eventually led to an explosion of data on the 'me' self (see Bracken 1996).

This explosion occurred after a long period that was dominated by functionalist behaviourism. Under that paradigm the self was not considered at all. It was not until the cognitive 'revolution' emerged in the 1960s, along with the increasing popularity of social psychology, that the door was opened for the re-admittance of the self back into psychology at large. Under the discourses of modernity, the self was conceptualized as unitary, autonomous and machine-like. Behaviourism's complete rejection of the self was cause for alarm amongst leading psychologists. As a result, Gordon Allport made a plea that initially fell on deaf ears: for the re-admittance of the self into psychology. In his analysis of Allport's plea, Danziger notes that it was made: 'on the grounds that this concept was required in order to do justice to the unity and coherence of the human personality' (1997: 148). Prior to the 1960s there were some notable exceptions to behaviourism where the 'I' and 'me' selves respectively were considered. These exceptions came from some psychodynamic schools (for example: Adler, Jung, Horney, Sullivan, Erikson); Kelly's school of *personal constructs*; and the existential and humanistic traditions. Eventually new psychoanalytic schools emerged, which made extensive use of the self (for example, Kohut and *self psychology*). The 'cognitive revolution', which some consider as having unseated behaviourism as the dominant paradigm in academic psychology, produced some innovative theoretical work on the self, such as the theory of *self schemata* (Markus 1980). This paradigm retained the principle features of modernity such as unity and the machine meta-phor of the mind. For example, the mind was seen as unified by the notion of intelligence, and information processing was modelled along lines suggested by computer hardware and software.

For James the self also represented a sense of individual agency, crossed with a biological capacity to experience consciousness, a focal point of the mind. James's conceptualization was perhaps a way to bridge Cartesian dualism by reconciling Descartes's proclama-tion of the self as a rational and thinking entity: *cogito ergo sum* [I think therefore I am] with the embodied flesh and blood self as a material object. In outlining a complex dynamic of the self, James would hierarchically categorize the concept into three aspects to which the 'me' and 'I' selves would be subjected. These are: (1) the material self; (2) the social self and (3) the spiritual self.

At the bottom of James's hierarchy is the material self, that is our flesh and bodied foundation on which the other selves could be built. The next self up is the social self, to which the individual's uniqueness as recognizable to others would be constituted. James's oft-quoted phrase: 'a man has as many social selves as there are individuals who recognize him and carry an image of him in their mind' (1890: 190) sums up the role characterizations subject to the social self. It would be a function of the subjective 'I' self to seek coherence and continuity over time of the social selves, so that these diverse expressions could be sensibly accounted for in con-sciousness. Such diverse sets of experiences could therefore be sub-ject to the integrative function of the 'I' self.

The highest point in James's tripartite division of self is his notion of the spiritual self. He argued that this self should be cherished and rendered 'supremely precious' (James 1890: 203), responsible for our thoughts, impressions, intuitions and morality. Indeed, James had argued that the empirical emphasis being adopted as part of psy-chology's shift into late modernity should never trump the use of psychology as a moral tool for self-understanding. Here again we find his split allegiance to both Romanticism and modernity. In this regard, James influenced both subjectivistic phenomenology and objectivistic experimental psychology. This division, between sub-ject and object, has never been satisfactorily resolved within psy-chology. Indeed, many of the issues that James raised continue to haunt the discipline. For example, in the spiritual self, James put forward the romantic and unitary notions of self; in the social self he put forward the multiplicity and plurality of self as expressed in the diverse functions of roles. In this regard he foreshadowed many of the debates around the self and its possible erasure that occupy postmodern and poststructural thinkers; and in the material self he brought in the possibility of biological determinism, inasmuch as who we are is grounded in the physical body. This latter notion of self has been a central feature of modernist quests for the 'essences' of being. For example, bio-psychology seeks to reduce our understandings of self to, amongst other things, the influence of genetics and such essences as pre-natal hormones and their effects on the development of the brain.

James and global self-esteem

James's work on articulating the significance of *self-esteem* has also had a considerable impact on the psychological disciplines. A core feature of the self in the Jamesian sense is its own reflected valuation. All human beings apparently ascribe a felt sense of worth to themselves. He postulates a universal need for self-esteem on the basis of the relationship between *pretensions* and *successes*. However, contemporary thinking on his self-esteem prototype has been rendered problematic. James sets up a daily fluctuation of self-esteem around a core evaluation. He theorized that if an individual experiences successes that are equal to or greater than their associated pretensions, they will experience an acceptable or high level of self-esteem. However, should successes not meet up to one's pretensions (for example failing to achieve one's stated aspirations) then low self-esteem results.

Subsequent research on James's construct has encouraged an explosion of scales, tests, re-tests and so on related to self-esteem. However, many contemporary theorists have encountered difficulties in verifying James's hypothesis. Andrews (1998), in her evaluation of the literature on self-esteem, criticizes a Jamesian approach to global self-esteem as 'uni-dimensional', and points to research that suggests we may have positive self-esteem for certain self-views and negative self-esteem for others, multiple self-evaluations co-existing. This points to a plural and multidimensional view of self-esteem. In this regard, Andrews points to the insufficiencies of a Jamesian approach and comments on the need to consider a more socially inclusive understanding. She cites Cooley and Mead as two pioneers in sociology who broached the study of the self. In her tight summary of their respective contributions to an understanding of the self, Andrews writes:

Cooley's (1902) notion of the 'looking-glass self' focused on the importance of individual perceptions of others' appraisals for the way we think about ourselves. Elaborating on this theme, Mead (1934) put forward the idea that the attitudes and values of significant others as well as society in general are internalized and form the basis for a 'generalized other' which is used as a yardstick by which we judge ourselves.

(Andrews 1998: 340)

Cooley and Mead separately extended the social self that James had outlined. These theorists appropriated the self from psychology and made it a central feature of the symbolic interactionist school of sociology. In so doing, they emphasized the interpersonal aspects of the self rather than the intrapersonal aspects (for example internalized objects, as discussed in psychodynamic models of object relations). In symbolic interactionism, the self is seen as a social construction based on symbolic interactions, as expressed in linguistic exchanges between members of a group. A kind of mirroring takes place in these interactions, which led Cooley to postulate the 'looking glass self': Harter cites Cooley's famous phrase: '[e]ach to each a looking glass, Reflects the other that doth pass' (1996: 3).

The extent to which the relationship to others affects one's self-esteem points to the social and cultural values accorded to this construct. Indeed, this is a consistent theme across the works of James, Cooley and Mead. Contemporary critics of the centrality of self-esteem and the pursuit of improving it point out cultural implications for the construct. Swann (1996) offers provocative ideas in *Self-Traps: The Elusive Quest for Higher Self-Esteem*. Here the author argues that an authentic treatment surrounding the whole question of self-esteem is undermined by prevailing cultural norms in America. In another but consistent vein Lasch (1979, 1984) asserted that the western self is embedded in a culture of narcissism where its satisfaction (hedonism) becomes paramount. In disputing the universal 'need' for self-esteem, other theorists employ cultural psychology to verify these universal assumptions. Recent research suggests that self-esteem appears more important to western (individualistic) cultures than to eastern (particularly collectivistic) cultures. For example, social psychologists Heine *et al.* (1999) have compared prevailing social norms in their cross-cultural study on the question: 'Is there a universal need for positive self-regard?' They compared North Americans with Japanese and found that North Americans were influenced by the prevailing cultural individualism that has institutionally enshrined the pursuit of happiness. The authors write:

> Being happy is a basic value for most North Americans. The U.S. Declaration of Independence, for example, proclaims that the pursuit of happiness is a fundamental right of its citizens. Failing to be happy in North America implies that one has somehow failed to realize the cultural mandate.
>
> (Heine *et al.* 1999: 51)

Self-esteem in North America is correlated with the pursuit of happiness, inasmuch as this pursuit is socially constructed within these cultures. Consequently, there is a considerable amount of research in Anglo-American cultures that focuses on the relationship between self-esteem and depression. Beck (1967) is undoubtedly the most influential theorist in this area, having developed a system of cognitive therapy that seeks to root out negative self-attitudes that demoralize self-worth and subject the individual to depression. This mode of therapy has, when combined with psychotropic drugs, led to a decrease in depressive symptoms for a significant number of depressed patients (Kaplan and Sadock 1991). Consequently, there has been a push within Anglo-American psychology to develop these techniques into systems of brief therapy, which have become considerably popular in recent years. That Anglo-Americans respond to this type of treatment may say more about their cultures than about a universal conception of *the* human condition. Indeed, Heine *et al.* were able to establish that the matter is quite different in Japan. They note that in Japan the pursuit of happiness is seen as somewhat of an 'immoral doctrine' insofar as it threatens the collectivistic nature of that culture:

> Japanese tend to believe their happy experiences will soon come to an end, and are often concerned that they will have to 'pay' for their happiness later on to restore the sense of balance. Indeed, an expression that one often hears in Japan (particularly among women) is 'I am so happy I am afraid' (*shiawase sugite kowai*), emphasising the fear of this payback. Japanese are thus quite hesitant to focus or dwell on positive feelings.
>
> (Heine *et al.* 1999: 51)

They conclude: 'Asian cultures thus do not appear to cultivate the need to experience positive feelings about the self' (Heine *et al.* 1999: 52). Self-esteem as a feature of individualistic cultures must be balanced and understood through alternative paradigms, in this case collectivism. Words in Japanese approximating related terms, such as self-confidence (*jishin*), are understood through the cultural embeddedness of collectivism. Is self-esteem a culturally specific phenomenon? Culture, as it relates to self, appears to be a powerful influence. In considering the self it seems quite warranted that one investigate culture and its influence. Whereas in this book we focus primarily on Anglo-American and other western traditions, we also point out the cultural limitations of doing so in regard to self.

The critical turn

Late modernity arose as a result of the frustration that many had with the romantic and dreamy idealism that had captured the masses during the nineteenth century. As a result of technological advances, electricity, machinery, radio and other modern conveniences, a much more functionalist realism took over from a romanticism perceived by some as 'woolly minded'. In late modernity the prevailing beliefs were with science and its grand narrative of progress. A revival of Enlightenment values of rationality, reason, objectivity and so on would capture the public imagination and instil a renewed sense of faith in progress. For some this faith would be short lived. The 1960s saw the emergence of a set of discourses loosely referred to as *postmodernism* and *poststructuralism*. These two intellectual currents overlap; both have their roots in nineteenth-century philosophy (for example Nietzsche). Some have suggested that poststructuralism arose out of the humanities as a tool to deconstruct language, while postmodernism arose out of aesthetics and the critique of such areas as modernist architecture. Simultaneously, advances in the hard sciences were shattering long held beliefs and contributed to the theory of poststructuralism and postmodernism. For example, quantum physics would challenge and unseat Newtonian linearity as a dominant mode of reasoning in physics. Most recently, information technology has also been implicated in the shift towards postmodernity. In regard to technology, Lather writes: 'the information explosion which is the ground of postmodernism . . . [is] the latest stage of the Enlightenment . . . a rupture with that era and the beginning of a new age' (1991: 21). Both postmodern and poststructuralist critics call into question the claims of modernists to accurately represent universal truths. Such critics take issue with late modernity's claim to represent 'the real' accurately, neutrally and therefore objectively.

In psychology, functionalist behaviourism came to dominate most academic work in the discipline. Experimental psychology, which branched beyond behaviourism, continued to use the dominant objectivism which behaviourism extolled. Gergen (1991: 140) points out that experimentalists, as exponents of late modernity, conceptualized people in universal terms that were: 'reliable, predictable, and authentic'. Under modernity, the implicit claim was made that a true and solid, objectifiable self can ultimately be known. This contrasts with postmodern accounts that counter: '[w]hatever we are is beyond the telling' (Gergen 1991: 82).

Modernity produced campaigns based on the reliable, predictable and authentic self. Eugenics and behaviourism extended objectivist and functionalist principles to the next logical level. First, the self would be extinguished as a concept. Behaviour would be enshrined as the most important feature of humanity; knowing and controlling human behaviour took centre stage. Next, eugenicists purported to be able to control the human condition by eradicating undesirable elements from the gene pool. Behaviourists inaugurated programmes based on reward and punishment. Undesirable behaviours would be subjected to electric shock or nausea inducing drugs. Having done away with the deep, unknowable self, modernists felt secure in their beliefs that they could come to fully know and therefore control the human subject.

In this chapter we have posited the self as an evolving social and historical concept that affects the inner lives of those who carry its, at least partial, linguistic constitution. This is consistent with poststructuralist theory, which declares that the self exists only because there is a word to define it. Finke writes: 'like the conscious itself, [the self] is an effect of language, of enunciation' (1997: 125). Nevertheless, many poststructuralists are not inclined to accept the self, since for them it is a social construction created out of language, it has no absolute foundation. What then is its purpose? Foucault, argue McHoul and Grace (1993) would say that the construction of selfhood serves structural power relations based on domination, surveillance and coercion. This and other poststructural views point to the creation of the modern liberal self as a product of the Enlightenment and its associated individualism. Individual selves, of course, can only function if they are predicated on individual identities. Identities flow into the interconnections of race, culture, class, sex and sexuality. Perhaps this is where Foucault gains currency for his discourse on the *technologies of the self*. For example, if selfhood is constituted through historically emergent practices, one can look back and see such practices anew within a given social context. Dreyfus and Rabinow (1982) point out that Foucault's work identifies the *confession* as being a central technology of the self that arose by universal order of the Roman Church during the thirteenth century. In this vein, selves existed because they could confess and in so doing not just express the sinful self but also confess as an act of faith. Therefore, the self slowly began to emerge as not only outwardly and socially accountable but also inwardly accountable, to be made available for surveillance and consequent retribution for one's sinful inner thoughts and desires.

A Foucauldian analysis suggests that counselling and therapy are newer technologies of the self. People come to therapy because they have an inner self that has historically been named and institutionally trained to confess. Whilst individuals may feel somewhat uncomfortable with disclosure, it has become an integral part of the cultures from which we come. The therapeutic intervention 'tell me a secret', through the ethics of confidentiality, is a powerful new version of an old confessional theme. Jung (1961) understood this arrangement quite well and even deemed his entire mode of therapy his 'unique confession', which he said differed from the Freudian or Adlerian 'confessions'.

Dreyfus and Rabinow (1982: 175) further elaborate on the meaning of the technology of the self:

> The key to the technology of the self is the belief that one can, with the help of experts, tell the truth about oneself. It is a central tenet not only in psychiatric sciences and medicine, but also in the law, [and] education . . . The conviction that truth can be discovered through self-examination of consciousness and the confession of one's thoughts and acts now appears so natural, so compelling, indeed so self-evident, that it seems unreasonable to posit that such self-examination is a central component in a strategy of power.

No doubt we see Nietzsche's mark on Foucault in this confessional theme. The inherent subjectivity of the particular aspect under discussion is foregrounded as an artefact of its creator, theory as a feature of the self. Nietzsche similarly declared: 'it has gradually become clear to me what every great philosophy has hitherto been: a confession on the part of its author and a kind of involuntary and unconscious memoir' ([1886]1961: section 6).

Lacan and the other

Before moving on to the subject of personality, we will consider some of the implicit ideas around the self and subjectivity put forward by the psychoanalytic work of Jaques Lacan (1901–81). These ideas are presented separately from other psychoanalytic writings on self in this volume, because the Lacanian position is effectively a critique of the idea of self itself in addition to being a critique of aspects classical psychoanalysis and psychodynamic psychology. Lacanians generally distance themselves from the notion of self and prefer the idea of subjectivity as more consistent with their privileging of the unconscious.

There is no easy way to approach Lacanian and post-Lacanian discourse, and like the unconscious itself, Lacan's writing often defies a surface and readily acceptable understanding. It is opaque, contemplative and challenging. He decried the psychoanalytic shift to ego psychology and made an impassioned plea for 'a return to Freud', but rejected the metaphysical aspects of Freudian theory. Subsequently, having rejected psychoanalytic metapsychology (the tripartite division of id, ego and superego), Lacan re-read orthodox Freudian notions through the lens of structuralism, claiming that the unconscious is constituted like a language-based, rather than an essence-based, entity.

Lacan made a fundamental distinction between the flesh and blood penis and the *phallus*; the latter is constituted and internalized through language, which children incorporate as they accede to the *symbolic order*. In this process the phallus becomes the ultimate signifier of desire, which sets up a predominance of male signified sexuality and its gendered features. However, the phallus is never obtainable, it cannot be possessed because it is not a thing, it represents lack, for males as well as females.

The accession to the external symbolic order, predicated on the phallic 'law of the father', occurs alongside the development of a sense of separateness, of self. This occurs through mirroring, a stage in which infants come to know themselves as split subjects, through reflection in actual mirrors or through being mirrored by others (for example mother, the eyes of another). Tong interprets Lacan's theory in the following manner:

> For Lacan, the mirror stage is very significant, for it instructs us that the child must become two in order to become one. The self comes to see itself as a mirror image of its real self.

Lacan believed that this initial process of self-constitution serves as a paradigm for all subsequent relations; the self is always finding itself through reflections in the Other.

(Tong 1989: 221)

In the mirror stage, the infant's sense of being a subject is split since the self is aware of both being and not being the mirror image. The self develops out of partial identifications with images as seen by an other, and in this regard it is always imaginary. Benvenuto relates this identification with the myth of Narcissus:

The mirror is an orthopaedia of human power and beauty, in other words Narcissus falls in love with his own image . . . [the] split between one's own fragmented being and its reflection in the mirror constitutes a new psychic stage in the dialectic of separation/unification . . . The world is no longer an extension of the infant but is doubled; the other becomes a double of oneself. This relation with the double always provokes conflict, because if the other is a double of oneself he is also a rival. The mirror inaugurates a rivalry with oneself; the object of identi-fication also becomes an object of hatred and aggression.

(Benvenuto 1997: 29)

The other can reflect the contents of the unconscious through projection and transference, indeed Lacanians insist that: 'the un-conscious presupposes the other' (Geerardyn 1997: 160).

In invoking the 'phallus-as-lack' for both sexes, Lacan simultan-eously places 'it' (rather than the penis) as a central feature of the psyche. In this regard, Lacan views human subjectivity as gendered. By turning away from the ego, and therefore from consciousness, the Lacanian simultaneously turns away from any notion of 'self' as understood in ego psychology. The self becomes a construction out of mirroring, a fictionalized and un-reified signifier. The 'I' is only a function of grammar, designating both the speaker and the spoken: it produces an imaginary construct occupying a place in the sym-bolic order. Raoul translates Sylvie Le Poulichet's summary of Lacan's position: ' "I" = sédimentation of residue of narcissistic identifications' (1994: 16). Finke elaborates:

Poststructuralist analysis, particularly that dependent upon the works of Lacan, replaces terms like 'self' or 'individual' with their connotations of autonomy and unity with the term 'subject', which more fully captures the sense of subjection, of the self's fashioning by its insertion into an already articulated symbolic economy.

(Finke 1997: 125)

Finke's analysis is also consistent with Butler's reading of Lacan: 'the ego is a perpetually unstable phenomenon, resting upon a primary repression of unconscious drives which return perpetually to haunt and undermine the ostensible unity of the ego' (1990a: 328). Lacan was opposed to North American ego psychology, viewing their 'reification' of the ego and its diminishment of the unconscious with disdain. He also opposed the Kleinians and British object relations theory for their 'idealization' of motherhood and subsequently their privileging of the breast over the penis, both of which, for Lacan, are subservient to the phallus. The matter becomes somewhat confused, however, when we look at Kleinian theory, which suggests that the breast can be unconsciously imaged as a substitute penile object (Laurent 1997).

Some post-Lacanians have opposed Lacan's 'phallocentrism' and sought to conceptualize the person, particularly women, in ways that are independent from the phallus. Irigaray, for example, conceives of a way for women to circumvent the phallus through her notion of the *feminine/feminine*, which Tong summarizes as: 'a way to bring women to selfhood and language that does not have to be mediated in any way through men' (Tong 1989: 226). For Irigaray the issue centres around breaking women away from an identification with absence/lack and conceptualizing new metaphoric alternatives to Lacan's Imaginary and Symbolic orders.

Personality and character

Our discussion of the self has thus far excluded those specific facets that bring uniqueness of expression to this construct. Those in the psychological traditions generally agree that there are complex issues surrounding the self and its uniqueness of expression that warrant detailed investigation. It is the what, why and how this is the case that form the basis of disagreements across various schools of personality. Indeed, Locke set the stage long before the birth of psychology as a distinct discipline when he wrote about the person: 'a thinking intelligent Being, that has reason and reflection, and can consider itself as it self, the same thinking thing in different times and places' (cited in Woolhouse 1995: 494). The 'same thinking thing' assumes some durability of uniqueness over time. Personality theories have traditionally set out to enquire about and describe those assembled qualities and characteristics that lend distinctiveness to individuality. In this sense, personality, as traditionally operationalized in personality psychology, has sought to identify enduring traits that lend originality to human subjects.

One notices that it is more common to speak of personality these days than to speak of *character* as in earlier times. The distinction between the two is generally espoused on moral terms. Crisp writes: '[c]ultivation of good character is seen as pivotal to moral life, and an understanding of character provides a standpoint for ethical criticism of oneself and others' (1995: 129–30). However, the term 'character' in the English language is also somewhat overburdened. The *Oxford English Dictionary* cites 19 different definitions for the word. For our purposes, the definitions numbered 8, 11 and 14 seem relevant for repetition: (8) 'A distinctive mark, evidence, or token; a feature, trait, characteristic'; (11) 'The sum of the moral and mental qualities which distinguish an individual or a race, viewed as a homogenous whole; the individuality impressed by nature and habit on man, or nation; mental or moral constitution'; (14) 'A description, delineation, or detailed report of a person's qualities'.

Character seems to involve an etching or 'distinctive mark' that endures over time and lends a person distinctiveness, coherence and continuity. Hillman (1999) describes character as bedrock, something that is constituted by deeper form, a structure less resistant to change over time than implied by *personality*. Consistent with this meaning of 'character' is the possibility of identifying types of form. For example, the creation of taxonomies, which organize and present character in a consistent and enduring manner known as *typology*. Character typology (for example, Jung's) has been used to generate general and universal patterns that have captured many empirical imaginations in psychology. These ideas are where critics locate their bases of disagreement. As a reflection of the perspectivism that has been revealed under current intellectual trends, a single monolithic, foundational and absolutist notion of character (as frequently portrayed in character typology) appears problematic. Moreover, the moral nature of the word character invariably points to the thorny question: 'whose ethics, whose morality?'

The overlap between the notions of character and personality is obvious. Both terms imply a stable structure of personal distinctiveness. This structure may be conceptualized on a continuum: from plural and infinitely mutable through to hard and constituting reliability and therefore predictability over time. We might ask, to what extent is our distinctiveness endurable and therefore measurable? Indeed, it is difficult to speak of *personality structure* as distinct from the frame of reference used to view such 'structures'. This frame of reference is often the individual who posits a personality theory. The many competing models of personality to be explored in this book only accentuate this point. Are personality theories only the stuff of one's own confessional, regardless of the application of scientific methods to these elements? Perhaps the starting point for unravelling the puzzles of character and personality is the theorist's own life experiences. In rational emotive behaviour therapy, Albert Ellis describes how he overcame his own sense of inferiority about dating women by using the principles of rationality (Velten 1998). His system developed out of his own lived experience. However, academic psychology has also sought to identify and validate personality traits that are independent of a given individual's bias, indeed for many in psychology this is essential, a rule of good science.

The distinction between an experimental psychologist's search for personality/character traits and the *personologist's* search for an understanding of human lives seems important. Experimental psychology is rooted in positivistic assumptions of a stable, natural and knowable world that can be revealed through the methods of science. This modernist stance argues that traits are pre-existent (such as Eysenck's introversion-extroversion) and biologically grounded to serve the evolutionary needs of an organism. To distinguish between this approach and those that seek a more holistic understanding of personality, we might want to examine briefly the notion of *personology*. In so doing, it is clear that personality and personology share significant overlapping interests (for example, in traits). Personologists such as Murray did not necessarily eschew scientific method, but the focus was certainly different from experimental psychology. Murray (1938: 4) offered his definition of personology:

> The branch of psychology which principally concerns itself with the study of human lives and the factors that influence their course, which investigates individual differences and types of personality, may be termed "personology" instead of "the psychology of personality", a clumsy and tautological expression.

Murray and other personologists such as Gordon Allport (1937) had a tremendous impact on the study of personality, particularly in

America. Allport inaugurated the formal study of personality through his trait scheme, based on what he called *heuristic realism*. This stand-point allows for error in studying personality on the basis that the individual is (apparently) in possession of real, knowable and endur-ing traits, traits being fundamental units that provide the individual human subject with consistency and unity. Traits are subject to the unity of the personality in motion, that is a person is always *becom-ing*. In this act of becoming lies the development of the self, for which Allport (1955) would apply the concept of the *proprium*: where individuals come to know that they are the person who *is*, knowing that one knows through reflection and continuity. The developing self is teleologically governed by the proprium, as long as the indi-vidual successfully develops through the eight stages that Allport outlined:

1 a *sense of bodily self*, which develops in the first year of life;
2 individual *self identity* follows in the second year;
3 *self-esteem* in the third;
4 *self-extension* from years four to six;
5 *self-image* develops simultaneously with self-extension;
6 *self as rational coper* from ages 6 to 12;
7 *propriate strivings* [life goals of the self] from ages 12 through the adolescent years;
8 *self-as-knower* emerges in adulthood as the sum total of all previ-ous self experiences.

Summary

The subject of self and personality is very complex. In this chapter, we have attempted to outline the history of concepts of the self and to visit some of the issues that have captivated personality theorists over the past century or so. Philosophy has been intentionally drawn into the discussion in order to illustrate the critical scrutiny to which the self and personality have been subjected. It is argued that both the self and personality are integral to (post)modern applications in the theory and practice of psychotherapy. The chapters that follow flesh out the specifics of the self within the context of personality, as represented in some leading areas of the discipline.

In proceeding with this study it might be useful to keep some conundrums in mind. We might ask: If we have a self and a person-ality, what happens to them when we become unconscious (for example coma)? This leads to a related idea: Is selfhood or personality entirely dependent on consciousness; can either exist unconsciously? Do they hide somewhere in the dark corners of the psyche? And what of the selves we were in youth, are we still the same? Does the self/personality change over time? If so, to what degree? What regulates change for the self and personality? And what of literary representations, do famous figures such as Jane Eyre and David Copperfield have a character/personality even though their fictionality renders their possession of a self impossible? And what of those individuals who, due to neurological pathology, have lost their memories? If the self functions to integrate a sense of 'I' and 'me' over time, what happens when that one factor that allows for temporal continuity (memory) is removed? Does this mean that one does not have a self anymore? Is there a definable and definite psychic space where self resides? Does this elusive phantom continue to slip through our grasp?

Psychoanalytic perspectives on the self: 'classical' models

The 'driven' self of Freud's metapsychology

Midway through his career as a clinician and theorist, Sigmund Freud noted wryly that his case studies often read more like works of literature than like 'scientific' papers. At the time Freud was struggling to articulate a 'general psychology' which, he hoped, might lend some coherence to his case histories. It might be said that, for Freud, the self was *'selbstverständlich'*, taken for granted as a given. His efforts were directed mainly at dissecting the psyche. Nonetheless, while a conceptualization of the 'self' was never central to any of the models he developed, it is not hard to see how each phase in Freud's theorizing has implications for an understanding of the 'self'. First we will outline the development of Freud's theory and then will discuss how the existence of a 'self' is implicit in both his theory and his technique.

In the first phase of Freud's work, that which Sandler *et al.* (1997) have referred to as the 'affect trauma' phase (1885–97), Freud was concerned with how he might help 'hysterical' patients who suffered from 'reminiscences'. Symptoms were understood as the result of repressed or 'strangulated' affects, which were unable to find normal expression and which then manifested themselves in psychopathological behaviour.

In his second, 'topographical' phase Freud gathered together several of the threads he had described in his earlier work and articulated the tripartite model of System Unconscious (*Ucs*), System Preconscious (*Pcs*) and System Conscious (*Cs*). This model held sway throughout the next phase of Freud's theoretical development, roughly 1897 up until 1923. In this topographical model, the therapist struggled to help material that had been repressed (and which therefore resided in the System Unconscious) to find its way into the upper levels of mental functioning (i.e. the System Preconscious and System Conscious). The repressed material was seen as derived from an unconscious, biologically-based, instinctual drive, the *libido*. Freud and his colleagues attempted to link particular phases of libidinal development with particular personality structures.[1]

However, it was not until the third, or 'structural', phase of Freud's psychoanalytic theorizing (which extended from the publication of *The ego and the id* in 1923 up until his death in 1939) that he began to give serious attention to the issue of an enduring self and personality structure. This was the phase in which Freud outlined how the hypothesized id, ego and superego interact with each other and with external reality.

Freud was forced to take the step from the topographical to the structural model by the fact that he repeatedly encountered patients who seemed to be divided against themselves, seeking help but also resisting it. The clinical phenomenon of an 'unconscious sense of guilt' forced Freud to make room for the superego and its complementary intrapsychic structures, the id and the ego.

In considering the place of the 'self' in Freud's theory it is particularly helpful and important to recall that the concepts which the English-speaking world has read about as 'id', 'ego' and 'superego' first appeared in German as *es*, *ich* and *über-ich*. Freud's translator, James Strachey, thought that the use of Latin equivalents for Freud's very ordinary German terms might add some scientific respectability to psychoanalysis. Unfortunately, Strachey's decision to use these Latin terms put the 'self' into the shadows. The result was a perspective in which three reified agencies struggled with each other. The sense of an overarching 'self', something which Freud's own descriptions of his clinical work demonstrate that he took as a given, was lost.

Freud's observation regarding the 'literary' character of his case histories demonstrates that, although he was struggling to create a 'general psychology' which could be used to describe and explain the mental phenomena he observed in his practice, Freud continued to relate to his patients as *people*, as *selves*. Patients were not just collections of unconscious instinctual drives and their derivatives; nor were they reducible to egos trying to mediate compromises between ids and superegos on the battleground of external reality.

They were people with personal histories, talents, weaknesses and so forth. Their personalities were essential components of their overall clinical pictures.

Thus, although the language of psychoanalytic *theory* prevalent during Freud's lifetime neglected issues of the 'self' and 'personality' in favour of unconscious drives, libidinal phase development, inter-systemic conflict, defence and symptom formation, psychoanalytic *practice* could not and did not forget that each patient brings to treatment a unique personality which interacts with the personality of the therapist, one 'self' interacting with another. Cohler and Galatzer-Levy have argued that psychoanalytic theory, or 'metapsychology', as Freud liked to call it, has tended to be mechanistic, reductionistic and limited. In their view, psychoanalysis has survived as a valuable intervention because 'the clinical theory of psychoanalysis describes human psychology in terms of meanings and motives' (1992: 430), concepts which themselves are intrinsically tied to the concept of the 'self'.

The ego and its functions: a step towards a self

As mentioned above, Freud's ([1923]1961) publication of *The ego and the id* (*Das ich und das es*) marked a major revision or amplification of psychoanalytic theory. Freud's own published work in the years that followed tended towards the 'large' issues of culture (e.g. *The Future Of An Illusion, Civilization And Its Discontents, Moses And Monotheism*) and away from the clinical issues that forced consideration of the 'self'. However, a number of other analysts from Freud's circle, notably Anna Freud, Heinz Hartmann, Ernst Kris and Rudolph Loewenstein, took it on themselves to flesh out the various functions of Freud's newly-hypothesized ego. Anna Freud's *The Ego And The Mechanisms Of Defence* ([1936]1966) was followed by Hartmann, Kris and Loewenstein's 'Comments on the formation of psychic structure' (1947) and Hartmann's 'Comments on the psychoanalytic theory of the ego' (1950a); these works began the job of describing, via its many functions, the structure that Freud had called the *ich*.

Anna Freud ([1936]1966) described various ways in which an individual, faced with inevitable conflicts between internal, internalized and external forces, might defend themself from the anxiety that would result should the instincts and their associated drives (in the id) produce ideas or behaviour which met condemnation from the side of either the superego or the external world. Her cataloguing of regression, repression, reaction formation, isolation, undoing, projection, introjection, turning against the self, reversal and sublimation provided a vocabulary that proved useful for describing these 'mechanisms of defence'.

Anna Freud was quite aware of the fact that 'mechanisms of defence' implied a defender; this was the ego. The functions of the ego went far beyond defence, however. As she later elaborated them (see her *Normality and Pathology in Childhood: Assessments of Development*, 1965), they included activities such as perception, motility, speech and language, attention, memory, reality testing and synthesis (the drawing together of the various strands of ego functioning into a well-integrated fabric of behaviour). Hartmann (1950a, 1950b) introduced the idea that the development of some ego functions was more a function of 'maturation' than of the drives or of defensive reactions to the drives. In addition, he pointed out how development itself imposes some strains upon the psyche, quite apart from 'conflict' (as that is seen in the 'structural' model of id, ego and superego).

It was Hartmann who suggested that the term 'ego' be used to refer to an objectively-described assemblage of mental capacities (including elements such as perception, memory, defence and synthesis) which stand in an intermediary position between the id, the superego and external reality. In contrast, he suggested that the term 'self' be used to refer to the narcissistically-cathected mental representation of a very different assemblage: the individual's experience of his 'body ego' coupled with his experience of the various (conscious and unconscious) psychological phenomena for which the terms id, ego and superego were created.

The ego psychology championed by Anna Freud and her colleagues also implied a 'self' in its recognition that several conflicts were intrinsic to the psyche and unavoidable. These conflicts (which she termed 'internal', and which she differentiated from 'internalized' and 'external' conflicts) were between (1) love and hate, (2) activity and passivity and (3) masculinity and femininity. In her view, every person (every 'self') grapples with the co-existence of both poles of these three dimensions. The fact that the co-existence of these trends is experienced as conflictual implies a cohesive (or at least cohesion-seeking) self, which struggles to encompass both poles, love and hate toward the same person, wishes to be passive along with wishes to be active, and 'masculine' wishes which compete with 'feminine' ones.

Kleinian object relations and the self

Melanie Klein and her colleagues took an approach to understanding their patients and normal development that was quite different from that used by the ego psychologists. Rather than focusing on either drive development or ego development, Klein and her colleagues concentrated their attention on the ways in which a person's relationships with others (and especially the *intrapsychic* relationships between the mental representation of the self and the mental representations of others) affected mental functioning.[2] Klein moved the focus of interest from the *drives* and their vicissitudes (Freud's emphasis) to the *objects* of the drives, the ways in which those objects gained internal psychic representation, and the ways in which the *relations* between these internal objects affected intrapsychic life (hence, the 'object relations' school of psychoanalysis).

Klein saw the transition from the 'paranoid/schizoid position' to the 'depressive position' as a watershed in normal development. In the paranoid/schizoid position, good objects and bad objects are kept separate and outside of the self. In the depressive position, there is a recognition that an object may be both good and bad, the good and the bad are not split into separate objects, and this more complex and ambivalent representation of the object is taken into the self. While Klein tended to use 'self', 'ego' and 'subject' interchangeably, she eventually described the 'self' as 'the whole of the personality, which includes not only the ego but the instinctual life which Freud called the id'; and she described the 'ego' as 'the organized part of the self' (Klein [1959]1975: 249). Like Freud, Klein was more concerned with dissecting the self, understanding what went on beneath the surface, than in understanding the self *per se.* Like Freud, she tended to take the existence of the self as a non-controversial 'given'. However, several analysts who trace their lineage to Melanie Klein subsequently have given special attention to the 'self'.

Esther Bick (1964) added to and modified earlier Kleinian thinking in her discussion of the place of the skin in early psychic experience. Bick saw the dichotomy between 'containment' and 'going to pieces' as important in the mental organization of the infant. Bick argued that it is an important achievement when the infant-with-mother is able to 'introject' (i.e. take into a primordial self) an external object. Implicit in this achievement is the establishment of a boundary between self and non-self. Bick (1968) suggests that the infant's experience of their own skin provides essential psycho-sensory data, which helps with the development of the capacity to introject. For Bick the experience of a 'self' is built on the abilities to introject and to contain representations of external objects. These abilities are associated with the ability to fantasize a containing space, and it is this containing space (built on psychic experiences of the skin) that makes it possible to differentiate self- and object-representations.

Fairbairn (1941, 1963) developed Klein's work but took as his point of emphasis the organization (or disorganization) of the individual ego. While classical psychoanalysts focused on how their neurotic patients struggled to tame their instinctual impulses, Fairbairn's work with more seriously-disturbed patients led him to put the issue of the ego's ability to maintain itself and its relationships with internalized objects in the foreground. For Fairbairn, the creation and maintenance of an integrated, stable self was the psychological task *par excellence*; while drives and their derivatives remained significant, they were insofar as they played a part in the creation and organization of a troika of egos: a central (conscious) ego attached to the ideal object, a repressed libidinal ego and a repressed antilibidinal ego. In Fairbairn's view, psychic health requires that the individual achieves a successful amalgam of these three.

Reich, *Charakterpanzerung* and the self

Wilhelm Reich's ([1928]1950) concept of *Charakterpanzerung* ('character armour') has much to do with the self insofar as it describes the way in which separate ego functions (including bodily functions such as motility and posture, as well as the more specifically psychological defence mechanisms) combine to create a kind of psychological 'suit of armour' which is both adaptive and highly resistant to change. In many ways Reich's metaphor approximates the concept of 'personality', albeit with an emphasis on the way in which personality structure functions to protect an individual from threats (from external reality as well as from internal anxiety).

In his best-known paper, 'On character analysis', Reich focuses on the problems faced when character armour becomes inflexible, for example, when the 'self' has ossified and can no longer respond to the shifting circumstances presented by maturation and/or environmental changes. His writings on technique demonstrate the difficulties faced in converting what has become an ego-syntonic but confining shell into an object of analysis and change.

In Reich's view, what begins as a neurotic symptom (and is experienced as ego-alien, an *illness*) sometimes is gradually 'so interwoven into the total personality as to [become] tantamount to character traits' ([1928]1950: 110). It is here that one finds Reich's appreciation of the 'self', for he sees 'the character, the specific mode or pattern of behaviour of a person, [as] the expression of his entire past' ([1928]1950: 111). All of the patient's characteristic modes of behaviour: 'The patient's manner of speech, the way in which he looks at the analyst and greets him, the way he lies on the couch, the inflection of his voice, the measure of his conventional politeness, and so on' ([1928]1950: 112) . . . become for Reich objects of analysis, or of 'character analysis', as he would put it. The goal of analysis becomes an alteration of character, of the 'self'. 'The neurotic character must be altered to the extent to which it forms the characterological basis of neurotic symptoms, and to the extent to which it conditions disturbances in the capacity for work and for sexual gratification' ([1928]1950: 122). Reich's psychoanalytic treatment is not aimed at isolated symptoms but at the much more pervasive elements of character which can be gathered together under the rubric of the 'self'.

The self in narcissistic and borderline pathology

While much of our discussion of this topic appears later in this volume (Chapter 4), it seems important to point out here that the attempt to address some of the special difficulties posed by patients whose 'selves' are particularly vulnerable to attack and/or fragmentation represents an important developmental step in psychoanalytic theory.

Both Sigmund and Anna Freud took it as a 'given' that the patients who presented themselves for treatment arrived with enduring, relatively stable constellations of bodily and psychic capacities and limitations. These were the '*ich*' of Freud's structural model, and the Freuds described how these selves struggled with the task of creating a workable balance between instinctual urges and intrapsychic or social prohibitions. Reich took a further step when he underlined the fact that the 'self' or 'character' adapts to meet the stresses and strains of intrapsychic conflict, creating a character that incorporates within itself many expressions of both intra- and inter-systemic conflict.

The line of thinking introduced by Fairbairn (1941, 1963) marked an important development in psychoanalytic theory. While drives

and their derivatives remained significant, they derived their importance from the part they played in the creation and organization of a
self that could integrate (or at least coordinate) its many components.

In more recent times Kohut (1971, 1977, 1984) (writing on narcissistic disorders) and Kernberg (1976, 1982, 1995) (writing on borderline conditions) have emphasized that the 'self' is more than a set of
character traits which mirror the intrapsychic and external conflicts
faced by an individual. To them, the 'self' is a psychological object
in its own right, an object that has a developmental history of its
own and which can pose special technical problems in treatment.
To put this in somewhat different terms, they see the 'self' not as an
epiphenomenon floating atop a sea of drives, conflicts and defences,
but as an important contributor to how these drives and conflicts
are experienced and to how the defences are organized. We shall
have much more to say about Kohut and Kernberg in Chapter 4.

Summary

This chapter describes how 'classical' models of psychoanalysis
approach the 'self'. Generally speaking, Sigmund Freud assumed the
existence of the 'self' and its integrative functions but was far more
interested in elaborating a general psychology that gave primacy
of place to instincts, drives and the unconscious. Over time he recognized the need to include in his model the enduring, conscious
and preconscious modes of behaviour and thought to which he
gave the name, *'Das Ich'*. This psychic agency was, for Freud, the
mediator between the peremptory wishes of *'Das Es'* (the 'it' or id),
the proscriptions of *'Das Über-Ich'* (the 'over-I' or superego), and the
realities imposed by the external world.

Anna Freud and her colleagues elaborated many of the functions
of the ego, giving special attention to the many different strands
that contributed to it over the course of development. Their primary
focus remained on the drives, however, and they tended to see the
ego mainly as reacting to forces impinging upon it. One task that
Anna Freud assigned to the ego, that of *synthesis*, represents her
acknowledgement that there is a need for some overall orchestration
of the vectors which Sigmund Freud outlined in his structural model.

Klein directed her interest and emphasis not to the drives but
to their objects; she saw object relations as the crucial organizers
of instinctual wishes, fantasies and defences. Her emphasis on the
internal, mental representations of objects (including the self)

implies a container for these representations, but, like other psycho-analytic theorists of her era, she took the 'self' to be *selbstverständlich* (self-evident).

Reich's concept of 'character armour' is one specific, defensively-oriented representation of the 'self'; it proved to be an important contribution to psychoanalytic theory and technique. However, Reich's perspective remained rooted in drives and defences. The character armour worn by the 'self' was an object of analysis but the self was not yet seen as having a developmental momentum or significance of its own.

Clinical conditions which since have come to be labelled as 'narcissistic' and 'borderline' pathology were evident to Freud and the other 'classical' psychoanalytic theorists. However, they tended to view these conditions through the limited spectacles of drive theory. Likewise, the disorganization of schizophrenia and the withdrawal of psychotic depression were seen as failures in the cathexis of objects. It remained for later theorists (such as Fairbairn, Kohut and Kernberg) to address the 'self' as an object of clinical concern in its own right.

Psychoanalytic perspectives on the self: 'developmental' models

The segregation of psychoanalytic perspectives on the self into chapters devoted to 'classical' and 'developmental' models is quite obviously artificial. *Every* psychoanalytic perspective includes important developmental aspects. Nonetheless, there are a number of psychoanalytic theorists who have given special attention to the processes involved in early development and their relationship to the 'self'. We examine eight of these in this chapter.

Early organizers of experience (Spitz)

René Spitz began his observational studies of early childhood development in Europe during the Second World War and continued this line of work in Denver (Colorado, USA) through to the 1960s. Spitz perhaps is best known for his descriptions of marasmus and 'hospitalism'. It was Spitz who described how some infants would, when deprived of maternal care and handling, curl up and literally die despite the fact that they had access to adequate food, clothing and shelter. Spitz's films of children who had been hospitalized for long periods demonstrated massive developmental delays. His work found a timely echo in Harry Harlow's experiments with rhesus monkeys.[3]

Spitz's work demonstrated how the absence of maternal ministrations could have devastating effects on infant development. However, Spitz was also interested in normal development. His later research (1957, 1965) focused on the first year of life and outlined several crucial developmental steps. These were the social smile

(~3 months); stranger anxiety (~8 months); and the child's use of the gesture 'No' (~12–15 months).

Spitz demonstrated how these observable phenomena signalled important steps in the development of the infant's relationship to his caretakers and to the world around him. To Spitz the social smile did *not* suggest the beginning of an 'object relationship' between infant and caretaker but instead an early effort on the part of the infant to establish some kind of reciprocity with their environment.[4]

Spitz did not believe that the 3-month-old infant was able to direct a smile from their 'self' to an 'other', he thought the infant incapable of a distinction between these two concepts. Nonetheless, he considered the social smile an important step or 'organizer' on the way to true reciprocity.

In Spitz's model of development, stranger anxiety (sometimes called eight-month anxiety) is the second 'organizer' of the infantile psyche. It 'signals that the child has singled out the face of his mother and conferred on it a unique place among all other human faces' (1965: 161). To Spitz this was evidence that the infant has established a stable mental representation of the object, a representation which can be differentiated from other objects. Stranger anxiety demonstrates that 'the child has found *the* partner with whom he can form object relations in the true sense of the term' (1965: 162).

Spitz's third 'organizer' appears when the child first begins to indicate, by gesture or word, their refusal to accept some of the restrictions or deprivations imposed on them by their caretakers (Spitz 1957). The young child's 'No' represents an attack directed against the external world. Not only does this action further solidify the boundary between 'self' and 'other', but it demonstrates the child's new ability to use symbolic communication, another crucial step in normal development.

Each of Spitz's 'organizers' has implications for the 'self'. They mark growth in the ability to perceive boundaries, to establish enduring mental representations of self and others, and to communicate across the boundaries between self and others.

Pathological and normal development of the self in childhood (Mahler)

Like Spitz, Margaret Mahler (1968) began her study of early development by trying to understand early psychopathology. Rather than maternal deprivation, however, Mahler turned her attention to 'infantile autism'. Her observations of autistic children and their interactions with their mothers helped her to identify some crucial developmental steps upon which many autistic children stumbled. This led her and her colleagues to a series of studies on early development in normal children. The data they gathered led to their ground-breaking volume, *The Psychological Birth of the Human Infant* (Mahler *et al.* 1975).

Mahler described, in affectively-charged language, six phases of infant development which demonstrate the child's gradual movement from the almost totally dependent and undifferentiated state of the new-born to the relative independence of the 3-year-old child.

The first two phases, *normal autism* (0–1 month) and *normal symbiosis* (1–4 or 5 months), reflect Mahler's early interest in children with pervasive developmental disturbances. To Mahler, the observational data she and her colleagues gathered suggests that normal infants are unable to differentiate 'self' from 'other' during these early months of post-uterine life.

However, evidence of a process of gradual differentiation begins to appear at about five months of age. This process, which continues through the first 18 months, is marked by the use of transitional objects, a 'checking-back' pattern of interaction between child and mother, the emergence of reactions to strangers (including stranger anxiety), and the child's specific attachment to mother, with a specific smile reserved for mother alone. Mahler refers to this cluster of behavioural events as *hatching*.

Hatching is followed by *practising* (a process especially obvious between 10 and 12 months and 16 and 18 months). The newly mobile toddler often seems elated and caught up in a 'love affair with the world'. However, many children of this age and phase were noted to react to mother's absence by retreating to a low-keyed, cautious pattern of behaviour that looks nothing like the 'love affair' which was so obvious in mother's presence.

Mahler *et al.* (1975) noted that three separate strands are involved in this phase of development. First, the young child goes through a period of rapid body differentiation from mother. At the same time, however, the child makes it clear that mother has a special place in their heart (and therefore psyche). The child's ego functions develop quickly, but they continue to require the mother's proximity in order to function reliably.

Practising is succeeded by *rapprochement* (a phase beginning at 15–18 months and continuing in various derivative forms for many years). Prior to rapprochement the toddler is seen to dart away from mother, but then just as suddenly returns; they sometimes shadow mother closely and it becomes clear that they realize that it is possible to lose both mother and her love. A metaphor for this behaviour might be a rapidly-fading photograph, the toddlers are able to take an image of their mother with them as they explore the world around them but the image fades and, at a certain point, they must rush back to see mother 'in the flesh' again and to 'recharge' their mental image of her.

In the rapprochement phase proper some of the toddler's earlier excitement about being on their own feet appears to wane and there is a shift; the child becomes more aware of (and capable of) *social* interaction. Growth in communication abilities is both dramatic and pivotal as the child learns that they now are able to influence others and to do something about their growing separation and independence from mother.

The final phase that Mahler *et al.* focus on is one in which the child appears to consolidate the many strands of development into a sense of individuality (a 'self'). This includes the beginnings of libidinal object constancy and of gender identity. The child's understanding of spatial and temporal relationships allows them to talk about past and future events as well as the present. These same verbal abilities help them to talk and think about people who are not present, and about their 'self'.

While Mahler's outline of early development does not put the 'self' front-and-centre, it is easy to see that both her metaphor of 'hatching' as well as her conception of 'psychological birth' (involving progressive movement from an undifferentiated, 'autistic' state through symbiosis and on to an individuated state) imply a developing sense of 'self'.

Ethological perspectives on the development of the self in childhood (Bowlby, Ainsworth)

John Bowlby's trilogy of *Attachment, Separation* and *Loss* (1969, 1973, 1980) is an impressive attempt to coordinate data from several different perspectives: ethology, systems theory and psychoanalysis. Bowlby puts the phenomenon of the infant's *attachment* to the mother at the centre of his theorizing. Attachment, as a psychological entity, develops out of five biologically-based 'response systems' which are visible in the young child: sucking, crying, smiling, clinging and following. These evolutionarily moulded response systems are designed to elicit complementary responses from mother; and these maternal responses then loop back to affect the child's developing systems (including their internal working models of self, of mother and of their pattern of relating).

In some ways it would be accurate to say that Bowlby sees the development of the 'self' as an evolutionarily-determined phenomenon that contributes to the survival of the individual in so far as it helps to facilitate smooth reciprocal interactions between a young child and their mother. However, the 'self' that results is not necessarily or even usually a unitary phenomenon. Bowlby recognizes that an individual often has more than one model of behaviour that provides psychological orientation, and that these models may not be congruent with each other. This is, at least partly, due to the fact that memories are stored in both episodic and semantic forms. Semantically-stored information may not be consistent with episodically-stored information. Bowlby suggests that it is this discrepancy which leads to the common clinical observation that there are often 'gross inconsistencies between the generalizations a patient makes about his parents and what is implied by some of the episodes he recalls of how they actually behaved' (1980: 62).

Bowlby suggests that:

> In most individuals . . . there is a unified Principal System that is not only capable of self-reflection but has more or less ready access to all information in long-term store. . . . [However,] there are other individuals in whom Principal Systems are not unified so that, whilst one such System might have ready access to information held in one type of storage but little or no access to information held in another, the information to which another Principal System has . . . access might be in many respects complementary. The two systems would then differ in regard to what each perceived and how each interpreted and appraised events.
>
> (Bowlby 1980: 63–4)

The developmental psychologist Mary Ainsworth (1973) took Bowlby's concept of an ethologically-derived 'attachment' between infant and mother and put it to empirical test. Her main tool was the 'strange situation', a carefully-staged sequence of events designed to stress a young child [by putting them in close proximity to a stranger, first together with mother, then alone and finally in reunion again with mother]. Ainsworth used the strange situation to illuminate some characteristics of the child's relationship with their mother, especially four patterns of attachment, which they labelled 'secure', 'anxious-avoidant', 'ambivalent-resistant' and 'disorganized'. Ainsworth has demonstrated that these patterns have predictive value for later behaviour over a span of many years.

Like Bowlby, Ainsworth does not focus specifically on the 'self' as an object or psychic construct which plays a part in 'attachment'. However (and also like Bowlby), it is easy to see that the patterns of attachment that she describes imply both a 'self' and an 'other', as well as enduring mental models of how these two entities relate to each other. For example, a child who displays a 'disorganized' pattern of attachment appears to be caught in an approach/avoidance conflict; the child fears being separated from their caretaker, but equally fears being near her. The child's 'self' is doubly vulnerable, they may be abandoned or attacked.

Psychologically speaking, the significance of Ainsworth's patterns of attachment goes far beyond what the patterns suggest about the child–parent dyad. These patterns become the building blocks for the development of enduring internal working models which, in both cognitive and emotional domains, affect all future relationships between 'self' and 'other'.

Mother–infant interaction and the organization of the self (Emde, Stern)

Robert Emde has continued the work begun by his mentor, René Spitz, in an elegant series of studies that are remarkable for their multidisciplinary breadth and depth. His work combines perspectives from basic brain research, neural networks, systems theory, ethology, genetics and behavioural genetics, cognitive psychology and the socialization of emotion, as well as from his 'home' field of clinical psychoanalysis.

Emde's recent work (1999) revisits a concept that he introduced in the 1980s, that of the 'affective core of the self' (Emde 1983). Describing his earliest formulation, Emde recalls how he:

> proposed that each individual from early on gained a sense of continuity during developmental change throughout life because of an individualised and enduring pattern of affective monitoring . . . a patterned affective core of responsiveness provides each individual with an integrated sense of consistency,

allowing us, in effect, to know we are the same in spite of the many ways we change.

(Emde 1999: 323)

To this earlier conceptualization Emde now adds several additional elements. First, a broad range of research has demonstrated that the consistency provided by the affective core is the result of multiple, interacting processes rather than of a single, global process. Second, it appears that the emotional processes that help to form the affective core are not limited to brief, intense phenomena; indeed, it now appears that the majority of 'background' feelings are high in frequency but low in amplitude and therefore usually remain out of the realm of consciousness. Third, emotional processes interact constantly with memory systems and thus they take on a little different 'spin' every time they are evoked.

Were we to boil down Emde's intricate and wide-flung model to its essence, we might say that infants are born with a pre-adaptation to interaction with their caregivers. This pre-adaptation includes an ability to experience pleasure as well as an ability to attract and engage their caregivers. When infant–caregiver interactions are 'successful' (i.e. when they are able to match each other in content, rhythm, intensity, etc.), they provide both infant and caregiver with positive affective experiences. It is significant that these experiences occur in interaction with an 'other' and that aspects of these interactions are quickly committed to memory.

In 1988 Emde proposed that psychoanalytic researchers should attend not only to the ego but to the 'we-go', his neologistic label for an attuned infant–mother dyad able to accomplish the 'tasks' of infancy. Emde was applying Winnicott's well-known bon mot, 'There is no such thing as a baby' [in isolation from a mother], to his research. He noted that, 'While emotions from earliest infancy provide a sense of coherence for self-regulatory experience, this only occurs if there is a "self-regulating other"' (1999: 286) able to help the infant regulate him- or herself.

Emde thus defines the affective core of the self as 'An evolution-based species-wide capacity for emotional experience and expression [which] develops in the human being and gives us all a basic, consistent way of communicating with ourselves and with others' (1999: 323) By this he does not mean to invoke the concept of temperament. Rather, he argues that one's sense of continuity derives from an ongoing stream of low-level emotional processes (linked to procedural knowledge and other cognitive activities) which are largely non-conscious and automatic, becoming visible only when something interrupts the smoothly-running mental procedures involved in creating and maintaining the affective core.

For Emde, feelings are the 'glue' that allow a 'self' to develop. While feelings are experienced by the 'self', they are always and irreducibly interpersonal in nature. Although they have clear biological roots, they can develop only in an interpersonal context, a context that is active from the first days of post-uterine life (if not earlier) and which continues throughout the life span.

It is in the work of Daniel Stern (1985) that we finally encounter the 'self' placed centre stage. Stern draws on data from two directions, observations of normal infants and their caretakers, and clinical psychoanalytic work (mainly with adults). Each set of data has its strengths and weaknesses; Stern argues that each fills in gaps left by the other.

In Stern's version of the first three years of development, the infant progresses through domains of relatedness; these domains come to prominence in sequence but, once 'on stage', they remain present, active and in a continuous state of development.

In the first couple of months after birth the infant is busily engaged in noticing and committing to memory the relationships between the continuously-flowing elements of experience. Some connections are formed simply on the basis of temporal or spatial proximity; these reflect biases that are built into the infant's central nervous system. Other connections and integrations are less automatic, but the infant's marvellous capacity to detect patterns helps greatly with the organization of experience. Stern believes that a 'sense of an emergent self' is present and observable in this period.

As the infant continues to develop their sense of self, largely built on their experience of their body, its functioning and its interactions with the environment, they begin to add a second layer to their self which Stern calls a 'sense of a core self'. This comes on stage some time between 2 and 6 months of age and remains a presence throughout subsequent life. This 'core self' is 'a separate, cohesive, bounded, physical unit, with a sense of . . . agency, affectivity, and continuity in time' (1985: 10).

It is the emergence of the core self that permits the next layer of the self, which Stern calls the 'subjective self', to emerge, beginning towards the end of the first year. As with the prior layers (the 'emergent self' and the 'core self'), the subjective self remains on stage and active throughout the remainder of life. Its primary focus has to do with seeking and creating intersubjective relationships. That is, the child becomes able to recognize that they have a subjective life (thoughts and feelings), which may or may not be shared by others. This is a period of life in which the child oscillates between union with and separation from their caretakers (mentally, as well as physically).

Preverbal intersubjective experiences eventually are joined by verbally-mediated relatedness; this is the point at which Stern sees the emergence of a 'sense of verbal self'. The acquisition of language facilitates the acquisition and sharing of knowledge, including knowledge about subjective states. The symbols of language make it possible to objectify the self and to be self-reflective.

Unlike others covered in this chapter, Stern puts the self and its development at the centre of his model. He also emphasizes the *intersubjective* matrix (of child with mother) that is necessary (but not sufficient) if the child is to add the verbal, the subjective and the core selves onto the biologically-founded emergent self of the neonate.

There are many points of congruence between Emde's and Stern's models of early development. Both make liberal use of data drawn from developmental psychology (an area with which many psycho-analysts are uncomfortable). Both emphasize the importance of the infant–mother dyad in normal development. Both are sensitive to the issue of 'attunement' between mother and infant and its impact on the child's developing 'self'. Stern, however, is eager to abandon earlier psychoanalytic models of development (especially those based upon drive and/or ego development). Emde, on the other hand, is more integrative in his approach and prefers to see historical continuities where Stern sees a revolutionarily new perspective that, if adopted, makes older models redundant.

The self across the lifespan (Erikson, Vaillant)

Up to this point, the various psychoanalytic developmental theories we have outlined focus their attention almost entirely on the first three years of life. Our final two contributors take a longer view, both of development and of the self.

Erik Erikson's earliest psychoanalytic work grew out of his work in a school setting. Together with Peter Blos Sr, he was hired by Anna Freud, Dorothy Burlingham and Eva Rosenfeld to work in the experimental nursery and elementary school they had established in Vienna in 1927. This work led Erikson to become interested in psychoanalysis and he subsequently completed his analytic training in Vienna before emigrating to America in 1933. Erikson spent the next 40 years as a peripatetic academic and sometime clinician, at Harvard, Yale, the University of California (Berkeley) and the Austen Riggs Center.

Erikson's interests were broad and he contributed to a number of ground-breaking studies of normal development in children and young adults. He had a special interest in the overlap between psychoanalysis (which, at the time, was concerned mainly with drive and ego development) and cultural anthropology.

Erikson's most influential work, *Childhood and Society* ([1950]1963), represents his attempt to broaden the then-dominant psychoanalytic theories of development with observations and theories derived from cross-cultural observations of development.

Erikson emphasized that any approach to human behaviour and development must take into account the three domains of body (soma), psyche and society. Each played an essential role and none could be left out. Erikson took the classical libidinal phases of psychoanalytic drive theory and paired them with psychosocial tasks, each stated in terms of a polarity. He also extended development beyond the classical libidinal phases (oral, anal, phallic, latency and genital) and broadened the labels he gave to each developmental stage in a way that incorporated social and cultural issues (see Table 3.1).

Erikson's work struck a responsive chord in the America of the 1950s and 1960s, especially his description of the 'crisis' of adolescence as a conflict between 'identity' and 'identity confusion'. It is in this phase, and Erikson's writing about it (1968, 1982), that we see his concern with the self most clearly reflected.

> [In adolescence] a pervasive sense of identity brings into gradual accord the variety of changing self-images that have been experienced during childhood . . . and the role opportunities offering themselves to young persons for selection and commitment. On the one hand, a lasting sense of self cannot exist without a continuous experience of a conscious 'I,' which is the numinous center of existence: a kind of *existential identity*, then, which . . . must gradually transcend the psychosocial one.
>
> (Erikson 1982: 73, original emphasis)

In Erikson's view, development continues throughout life, and the 'self' continues to change over time.

Table 3.1 Erikson's stages of psychosexual development

Stages	Psychosexual stages and modes	Psychosocial crises
I Infancy	Oral-respiratory, sensory-kinesthetic (incorporative modes)	Basic trust vs. basic mistrust
II Early childhood	Anal-urethral, muscular (retentive-eliminative modes)	Autonomy vs. shame and doubt
III Play age	Infantile-genital, locomotor (intrusive and inclusive modes)	Initiative vs. guilt
IV School age	'Latency'	Industry vs. inferiority
V Adolescence	Puberty	Identity vs. identity confusion
VI Young adulthood	Genitality	Intimacy vs. isolation
VII Adulthood	Procreativity	Generativity vs. stagnation
VIII Old age	Generalization of sensual modes	Integrity vs. despair

Derived from Erikson 1982: 32.

George Vaillant (1977) bows to Erikson (as well as to Anna Freud, Harry Stack Sullivan and Heinz Hartmann) in his volume, *Adaptation to Life*. This is Vaillant's summary of the research findings of the Grant Foundation study that took as its population of developmental interest a cohort of 268 men who began their studies at Harvard in the late 1930s. Vaillant's reference to Erikson notes that it was Erikson's *Childhood and Society* that first provided 'convincing evidence that adults mature as well as children' (Vaillant 1977: 44).

Vaillant's work also demonstrates that adults mature in ways that reflect their prior adaptations. He outlines 18 basic adaptive mechanisms and demonstrates that an individual tends to use a particular subset of these mechanisms over the lifespan. At the same time, some of his subjects underwent startling changes and evolutions. Both stability and change pose challenges to the 'self'.

Vaillant does not address the 'self' directly. Instead, he contrasts the 23 men whose childhoods were objectively most bleak with the 23 whose childhoods appeared most sunny and notes that:

> four predictions could be made about the effect of childhood upon midlife adjustment. First, men with unhappy childhoods would be unable to play. Second, they would be dependent and lack trust in the universe. Third, they were more likely to be labelled mentally ill. Fourth, they would be without friends.
> (Vaillant 1977: 285)

The line of thought here, which relates to the 'self', is that the men of the Grant Study could be described in terms of 'character-istic reaction patterns to stress' (1977: 369). That is, they generally developed stable ways of coping with the 'slings and arrows of out-rageous fortune', with varying degrees of success and failure when viewed from the outside. No single event, however powerful and 'traumatic', was likely to mould an individual life. At the same time, it was clear that the ongoing interaction between an individual's choice of adaptive mechanisms and his relationships with other people has a powerful impact on 'adjustment'.

While the work of Spitz, Mahler, Bowlby, Ainsworth, Emde and Stern helps us understand the self in terms of its genesis and early organization, Erikson and Vaillant provide a crucial reminder that the 'self' is a 'work in progress' that can and must be nourished and re-formed throughout the lifespan.

Psychoanalytic perspectives on the self: late twentieth-century theory and technique

In Chapters 2 and 3 we have outlined psychoanalytic perspectives on the self which are derived from classical drive theory, from so-called 'ego psychology', and from various strands of developmental research.

In this chapter we examine ways in which psychoanalytic clinicians who work with patients whose problems lie outside of the 'neurotic' domain have come to think about the self. Heinz Kohut and Otto Kernberg represent two particularly important lines in the development of psychoanalytic theory. Kohut was particularly concerned with the treatment of the so-called 'narcissistic' personalities while Kernberg focused on work with 'borderline' patients.[5]

What Kohut and Kernberg have in common is a concern for the ways in which early experience can interfere with the development of a normal, cohesive and vital self. Their theories regarding such developmental pathology diverge, however, and so do their recommendations for clinical work with such disorders.

Kohut and 'self psychology'

A segment devoted to 'self psychology' within a book entitled *The Self and Personality Structure* is somehow reminiscent of the familiar Russian dolls that nest, one within another, in an ever-diminishing series. Nonetheless, this section deserves its heading: Heinz Kohut (1971, 1977, 1984) put the 'self' at the centre of both his theoretical and his technical writing. And, it is fair to say, no other author writing from a depth psychological perspective has focused on the vicissitudes of the self more than has Kohut.

Paradoxically, however, Kohut explicitly avoided a definition of the self, fearing that any such definition would lead to the kind of reification that has dogged Freud's (or Strachey's) 'ego'. Instead, he approached the topic from several different angles, offering what amounted to a sequential triangulation and 'location' of the self, without ever pinning it down completely.

In Kohut's writing the self is sometimes an agent, a doer of deeds; at other times it is something that has been created and which persists as a kind of mental structure. However, regardless of whether it is seen as active or reactive (or both), the self always requires interaction with other selves; for there can be no self without an other.

Approaching the self from a developmental perspective, Kohut argued that normal human infants are born with a *nuclear self* already in place (a biologically determined psychological entity). The interaction between this *nuclear self* and the *virtual self* (an image of the newborn's self, which resides in the minds of the infant's parents) will, under optimal circumstances, lead to the child's gradual organization of a *cohesive self*.

The *cohesive self* is preceded, however, by the *grandiose self*. This is the self that emerges out of the normal infantile experience of oneself as the centre of all experience, omnipotent in the control of everyone and everything before him. In normal circumstances, the infant's *grandiose self* interacts with the parents (their real behaviour as well as the virtual selves that they present to the infant) in ways that gradually and non-traumatically expose the infant to the facts that (1) he is not omnipotent and (2) his parents cannot insulate him from the normal frustrations of life. This process of gradual and titrated disenchantment requires that the infant's caretakers be empathetically attuned to the infant's needs.

Of course every parent, no matter how well attuned, will eventually (and repeatedly) 'fail' to be empathetically attuned. Under normal circumstances the infant is cared for by people who are 'good enough' at providing what the infant needs that the infant can set aside the grandiosity of infancy in favour of something more 'realistic', meanwhile constructing a self that is both vital and cohesive.

Kohut describes early interactions between the infant and his caretakers as involving the infant's 'self' and the infant's 'selfobjects'. In Kohut's vocabulary, selfobjects are mental representations created by the infant which reflect (to a greater or less degree) the ways in which the caretakers manage to admire, applaud, encourage, mirror and merge with the infant's own strivings.

Kohut sees the organization and maintenance of the self as *the* crucial psychological task facing the individual. This is first accomplished via interaction with others who are not yet seen as separate entities but as selfobjects.

> The *selfobject* is one's subjective experience of another person who provides a sustaining function to the self within a relationship, evoking and maintaining the self and the experience of selfhood by his or her presence or activity. Though the term is loosely applied to the participating persons (objects), it is primarily useful in describing the intrapsychic experience of various types of relationships between the self and other objects.
>
> (Moore and Fine 1990: 178)

Selfobjects are to Kohut's theory of self-organization what libidinal objects are to Freud's drive theory; selfobjects shape the infantile self through interaction with it. While Freud gave libidinal objects an important function in his metapsychology, he saw the drives as dominant in their relationships with libidinal objects and quite willing to accept substitutes; indeed, Freud saw the organization of libidinal drives and their channelling toward 'normal' libidinal objects as an immensely complex task which could easily go awry (Freud [1905]1953). Kohut sees selfobjects as crucial contributors to the organization of the self – an equally complex and sometimes problematic task that also can easily go awry.

To the extent that caretakers are able to function in particular ways toward the infant's *nuclear self*, they provide the raw material for the infant's experience of selfobjects and for the emergence of a series of self-selfobject relationships that eventually are organized into a set of fantasies, which then can provide sustenance to the self even when the original caretakers are no longer available.

For example, the early *merger* experiences characteristic of the infantile selfobject are succeeded (but not replaced) by *mirroring* selfobjects, which accept and confirm the 'grandness, goodness, and wholeness of the self' (Moore and Fine 1990: 178). Somewhat later in development, *idealized* selfobjects 'provide the experience of merger with the calm, power, wisdom, and goodness of idealized persons' (Moore and Fine 1990: 178).

Kohut's theory focuses on the impact of early infantile experience (both interpersonal and intrapsychic) on the emerging self. Thus it is more a psychology of *deficit* than of *conflict* (as the latter was outlined by Freud and the ego psychologists). Psychopathology, especially that involving disturbances in narcissism, reflects failures in early selfobject functions; in Kohutian theory these failures generally are laid at the feet of the infant's caretakers.

Kohut outlined several levels of self pathology, ranging from narcissistic behaviour disorders through narcissistic personality disorders on to borderline states and finally to psychosis. He saw the latter two diagnostic categories as generally beyond the power of psychoanalytic treatment. However, Kohut believed that the first two – the narcissistic behaviour disorders and the narcissistic personality disorders – were amenable to psychoanalytic treatment *if (and only if) psychoanalytic technique was tailored to fit these particular disorders and their particular vulnerabilities.*

Kohut's writings on treatment technique derive from his theory of pathogenesis. He highlights *empathy* as the tool *par excellence*, which allows the creation of a relationship between patient and analyst that can offer some hope of mitigating early self pathology.

Kohut suggests that, in treating such pathology, the therapist must constantly attend to and accept as legitimate the patient's expressed needs (e.g. for admiration). Such an attitude of acceptance encourages the emergence of selfobject transferences of two different kinds. One type, the *mirror transferences*, are related to the patient's attempts to stabilize a grandiose self that came to grief early in infancy. Another type, the *idealizing transferences*, represent an effort on the part of the patient to have the therapist take on some of the normal selfobject roles appropriate to early development.

Mirror transferences include merger and alter ego transferences, as well as mirror transferences proper:

> In the merger transference the analysand's grandiose self is supported by the idea of a single entity, the analyst-analysand. The alter-ego transference reflects the analysand's effort to maintain enhanced feelings of personal integrity through assumed similarity of ideals and intention. In the mirror transference proper, the analysand feels well because of the analyst's appreciative response to his grandiosity.
>
> (Cohler and Galatzer-Levy 1992: 441)

Idealizing transferences are those in which, in the patient's eyes, the therapist can do no wrong. Indeed, the patient uses the image of the idealized therapist as a way of helping the patient to feel vigorous, good and whole.

Kohut's therapeutic technique allows for long periods of time during which such selfobject transferences are allowed to develop. The analyst is seen as providing some elements of responsiveness to the patient's self, which are curative in themselves. This experience, shared by patient and therapist alike, puts the two of them in a good position to observe and attend to how the therapist's inevitable failures and insensitivities affect the patient's sense of self. It is through such experiences that:

> the analysand develops increasing capacity for managing this experienced failure without the loss of spontaneity and vigour of the self, which formerly characterized such disappointments. This capacity for resolving disappointments . . . results in what Kohut (1971) . . . termed a 'transmuting internalization,' in which functions previously performed by the external selfobject are . . . taken on by the analysand.
>
> (Cohler and Galatzer-Levy 1992: 442)

As is suggested by this line of thinking, Kohut sees the interaction between self and selfobject as remaining central to psychic health throughout the life cycle. Cohler and Galatzer-Levy note that:

> The selfobject world usually enlarges across the course of life, with lessened threat to the self caused by the loss of a particular selfobject. Rather than viewing development as a lessened need for self-object functions, there is a lessened vulnerability to the loss of any particular selfobject or a person in whom that function is embodied. *Whether there ever is a time when self-experiences are so solidly laid down as to be immutable to psychological stress is not clear.*
>
> (Cohler and Galatzer-Levy 1992: 444, emphasis added)

Kernberg and 'object relations'

Throughout the last quarter of the twentieth century Otto Kernberg (1976, 1982, 1995) has been one of the foremost writers in the area of the psychoanalytic theory of object relations. Kernberg has defined object relations theories as:

those that place the internalization, structuralization, and clinical reactivation . . . of the earliest dyadic object relations at the center of their motivational (genetic and developmental), structural, and clinical formulations. 'Internalization of object relations' refers to the concept that, in all interactions of the infant and child with the significant parental figures, what the infant internalizes is not an image or representation of the other ('the object') but the relationship between the self and the other, in the form of a self image or self representation interacting with an object image or object representation.

(Kernberg 1995: 450)

Obviously Kernberg's concern with 'object relations' includes and depends on his understanding of the 'self'. While Kernberg is only one of several other possible representatives of a modern object relations perspective (for example, Edith Jacobson or Margaret Mahler), we have selected him here because of his prominence and because he takes a 'middle' position that attempts to maintain links with prior psychoanalytic drive theory.

Kernberg approaches the topic of the self from an angle distinctly different from that of Kohut. While Kohut saw his formulations as making drive theory obsolete, Kernberg is at pains to integrate his theorizing with many aspects of classical drive theory. Secondly, Kernberg describes a constellation of affects which are not just discharge phenomena associated with drives; affects also represent certain aspects of the drive derivatives, which are embedded in the *relationship* between self and object representations. Indeed, Kernberg (1982) sees affects as in some ways *antecedent* to the drives; they assist in the organization of the biological phenomena underlying the drives into the psychologically coherent forces that Freud labelled 'libido' and aggression.

In Kernberg's view, there is no drive without an object and no object without a self. Drives do not exist in some abstract form; motivated by affects, they originate in a self and are directed toward an object, both of which contribute to the form that the drive derivatives take at any moment in time.

Working with 'borderline' and 'narcissistic' patients, Kernberg found himself drawn to the concept of a grandiose self which simultaneously contained aspects of a 'real self', of an 'ideal self' and of an 'ideal object'. Impulses and defences against impulses are not isolated in an autonomous self; instead, they find their expressions via internalized object relations, which include both self and object.

These object relations, in the borderline personality organization, often reflect pre-oedipal conflicts expressed in dissociated ego states that result from the use of 'splitting' defences. Affect states initially appear chaotic but, in treatment, gradually express themselves via a dominant primitive object relation which appears in the transference. This object relation includes both self and object representations, often expressed via an affect which bridges the two.

Kernberg's work with such patients aims at the analysis of the repeated and oscillating projections of unwanted self and object representations onto the therapist. These interact with their reciprocals, carried by the patient. (Thus the therapist may be imbued with 'witch-mother' attributes while the patient retains reciprocal 'fairy godmother' attributes.) The therapeutic task, then, is the gradual integration of the idealized and disowned (persecutory) aspects of these object relations into something more durable, complex and encompassing than the initial, split-off and polarized state of affairs.

One important technical consideration that both unites and differentiates Kernberg from Kohut is the importance each gives to the role of the therapist's responsivity to the patient. In Kohut's view, empathy is an essential component of the curative power of psychoanalysis. Kernberg takes another tack. He emphasizes how the therapist must be able to use his own responsivity to his patient to help him comprehend the patient's transferences. In Kernberg's vocabulary, it is the analyst's ability to analyse his own countertransference reactions to the borderline patient that enables the analyst to comprehend (and to empathize with?) the patient's defences, especially those which involve splitting and/or projective identification. The analyst's understanding and interpretation of these phenomena leads to a strengthening of the patient's ego.

In closing this chapter, which highlights late twentieth-century contributions to the psychoanalytic understanding of the self, we would like to take a moment to reflect on the development of psychoanalytic theory and technique over the span from Freud to the present.

Freud put biological instincts at the foundation of his structure and he remained preoccupied throughout his career with the ways in which these fundamental biological forces found psychological expression (as the drives, libido and aggression) in both individual lives and culture. He tended to assume that patients who sought his help had already achieved a coherent self, however that self might now be crippled as the result of unconscious conflict.

Freud left it to others to outline and detail the many ego functions that he took for granted in his patients. He vacillated back and forth between *Ich* and *Selbst* in a way that reflected his unwillingness to nail down this experientially rich and crucial concept.

The ego psychologists and developmental psychologists who followed Freud gradually produced a catalogue of terms that described the ego functions and the steps in their development, which could be observed from infancy onwards. They also described some of the crucial way-stations in the child's development of a sense of self, which was both differentiated from yet related to his or her caretakers.

As Modell (1985) points out, relatedness was not part of Freud's initial drive theory. However, attempts to apply psychoanalytic techniques to a widening scope of patients revealed that there were many people for whom both a sense of self and a sense of relatedness were highly problematic.

Kohut and Kernberg found it necessary to modify their technical approaches as they attempted to help these patients. Long periods of non-interpretive work were required in order to build a relationship between patient and analyst. Both Kohut and Kernberg saw the analyst as offering the patient a new object (or, in Kohut's vocabulary, a new selfobject) within a relationship designed to repair past deficits and failures.

Though both are concerned with the ways in which relationships between the child and others (especially early caretakers) affect the organization of the self, Kohut and Kernberg diverge in some important ways. Kohut sees aggression as a response to frustration while Kernberg sees it as an intrinsic aspect of human nature, founded in biology. Kohut sees intrapsychic conflict as theoretically avoidable (given optimal parenting) while Kernberg sides with Freud in his assessment that such conflict is unavoidable.

What is incontestable, however, is the fact that, by the end of the twentieth century, psychoanalytic perspectives on the self had developed and broadened far beyond where they had started a century before. What had begun at the end of the nineteenth century as an attempt to apply metaphors drawn from physics and physiology to the psychological symptomatology of middle-class Viennese society had broadened to a point where the 'four psychologies of psychoanalysis' (Pine 1988, 1990) now are seen as complementary partners. Drive psychology, ego psychology, object relations psychology and self psychology each have important insights to offer twenty-first-century clinicians, though the integration of these theoretical perspectives still remains somewhere over the horizon.

C H A P T E R **5**

The social and interpersonal self in Adlerian and neo-Freudian theory

From within psychoanalysis, the first shift towards the social realm and away from Freud's internal drive model, predicated on the sexualized libido, begins with Alfred Adler (1870–1937). Indeed, Adlerian theory goes beyond the psychoanalytic project and into humanistic, existential, cognitive, sociological and educational realms. Adler's general social and contextual views preceded his association with Freud as did his status as a pioneer of psychosomatic medicine. He also differed from Freud in emphasizing prevention through educational and coalitional approaches (stressing any combination of parents, teachers, physicians, social workers, counsellors, clergy and so on). For these and other reasons, Adler's school must be considered distinct from psychoanalysis, particularly in Anglo-American approaches, and an independent school in its own right (Micale 1993; Handlbauer 1998). Most Adlerians nevertheless, retain a broad psychodynamic identification. Horney, Fromm and Sullivan remain more orthodox to the umbrella of psychoanalysis and yet move in the Adlerian direction, towards the social world and its contextual interconnections with the interiority of the psyche. In remaining within the psychoanalytic movement, these theorists nevertheless critically challenge orthodox psychoanalytic premises.

Though retaining the unconscious, Adler was the first psychodynamic theorist to shift towards the ego and its constructions of unity. In this regard, the study of the self in psychodynamic terms begins with Adler. Two noted historians in psychiatry and psychoanalysis have credited Adler as the founding father of ego psychology and the first psychodynamic thinker to posit the significance of social context in the psychodynamic sphere (Ellenberger 1970;

Ehrenwald 1991). Moreover, the similarity of the self as conceptualized by Horney and Sullivan led Ellenberger to suggest that these theorists could be more accurately described as 'neo-Adlerians' than 'neo-Freudians'. None of these authors credit Adler or acknowledge the similarity in their theoretical claims. This is not surprising as the schisms and breaks that characterize the psychoanalytic discourses as a whole were such that reference to other figures generally took the form of a critique or polemic; differences rather than similarities were stressed. For example, Horney admits to having analysed herself using Adler's early concept of the masculine protest. She was familiar with Adlerian theory but never conceded a link: indeed she criticized Adler for failing to take a proper 'journey into the depths' (cited in Paris 1994: 76).

Alfred Adler and the self

Adler was, like Freud and James, a transitional figure between nineteenth-century Romanticism and late modernity. His views of self and comparable theory of personality are more strongly linked to late modernity and its associated functionalism than Freud's theory, although Freud too eventually turned his focus towards the ego. The clearest reasoning for Adler's early turn to the ego and away from the Freudian unconscious can be found in the demographics of his patient population (Hoffman 1994). Whereas Freud tended to work with middle- and upper-class patients, who could well afford a long analysis, Adler tended to work with the poor and working-class people of the Viennese suburbs. Those people needed quick solutions, which prompted Adler to devise a more active/directive approach similar to Socratic questioning (Stein 1991). Indeed, his specialization was in the arena of differential diagnosis where he had an excellent track record for distinguishing physical and psychical causes to symptomology.

Initially, Adler was a socialist and carried this reputation through the many years he was associated with Freud's Wednesday discussion group. He was a co-founder of this group where psychoanalysis was institutionalized under Freud's guidance. Adler was associated with the group from its inception in 1902 until his split with Freud in 1911. Following this split, Adler inaugurated an independent school, which he eventually called *individual psychology*. The name is not intended to detract from the social emphasis of the theory, but is rather derived from the Latin *individuus* meaning indivisibility. As a confession, Adler tells the story of his childhood fear of crossing a cemetery on his way to school (the story might have been a childhood dream as authorities were never able to verify the location of this cemetery). As a child, the fear and reality of death deeply affected Adler. His brother had died in early childhood in the bed next to him. Moreover, Adler was a very sickly child and had feared for his own mortality. Out of these fears, Adler would compensate by aspiring to become a medical doctor, of seeking to overcome his inferiority feelings. This confession says much about his theory of personality, towards what Adler called the *style of life*.

Perhaps Adler's most revered contribution, at least amongst Adlerians, is his concept of *gemeinschaftsgefühl* (Gr.) translated initially as 'social interest'. Decades later, this translation was corrected by Ansbacher (1999) (who had made the first translation under Adler's guidance) to be more consistent with its original meaning, 'feeling of community'. The theory posits that those who are experiencing mental health are able to contribute to the strengthening of community. Mental health and strong, cohesive communities are considered synonymous. Selfhood in the Adlerian scheme is intrinsically tied to community feeling. This implicitly leads to the critique of society for its lack of community feeling, for its individualism and consequent widespread feelings of alienation. Community feeling would only develop after the self-bounded individual is liberated, Adler wrote:

> Self-boundedness (*Ichgebundenheit*) is the central point of attack of Individual Psychology. The self-bound individual always forgets that his self would be safeguarded better and automatically the more he prepares himself for the welfare of mankind, and that in this respect no limits are set for him.
>
> (Adler 1956: 112)

Though retaining many of his socialist ideals, Adler turns more to the problem of existentialism in his late theory. In so doing he also retains several core psychoanalytic assumptions such as the role of the unconscious, the notion of repression, and the significance of the transference relationship in therapy. Adlerian theory emphasizes interpretation of unconscious life and the production of metaphor and imagery in conveying the *teleological* function of the psyche, that is, the purposeful and goal directedness of a given individual's *style of life*. For example, Adlerians emphasize the significance of dreams and the analysis of early recollections in shaping an individual's cognitions about self, the world and others. In extracting cognitive productions such as beliefs, Adler was able to analyse the patient and come up with their *unique law of movement*, that is the underlying goals of an individual's style of life. For Adler, the self carries uniqueness predicated on movement and striving.

Consonant with psychoanalysis, Adler's view of self emphasizes the formative years of childhood in forming one's style of life. In this regard he also stresses the psychodynamic significance of the *family constellation*. For example, selfhood is generally affected by birth order (first born, second, middle, youngest, only) and by the relations with parents. Other significant figures in the family generally leave an indelible impression on an individual's style of life (for example grandparents, pets). Establishing, analysing and making conscious the impact of the family constellation indicates much about that person's phenomenology and subsequent strivings to overcome unconscious *feelings of inferiority*. Adler hypothesized that at the core of psychic functioning lies a feeling of inferiority and that neurosis develops around associated complexes and compensations. He insisted that a striving to overcome felt inferiority is equivalent to a universal striving for perfection. In his clinical experience, Adler was consistently dealing with the romantic striving for perfection latently posited in his patients' goals. Such striving was evident in what Adler (1956) described as the 'neurotic personality'. This perfectionism amounted to a cognitive distortion of what a person could realistically achieve. In uncovering the *basic mistakes* of one's style of life, perfectionistic striving would be revealed. Compensation was posited as a means to express the disjunction between the ideals of an individual and the actual experience of failing to reach them. For many, psychosomatic complaints would surface as a meaningful but hidden language or *organ jargon*, that is the body would speak what the ego-ideal forbade (Linden 1997).

The notion of self or selfhood is central to the English translation of Adlerian theory and practice. In the English translation of Adler's distinct meaning of the German *Ich*, 'self' is emphasized rather than 'ego' as this translation more accurately represents what Adler means by *ich* (Ansbacher and Ansbacher, in Adler 1956). The established Adlerian canon on unity/holism suggests that the self is the outcome of a unifying function constituted by the style of life. In this regard, this unifying function is similar to the role of James's (1890) subjectivistic 'I' self. One's style of life serves as a reference for attitudes, reflexive views of self, others, the world and one's own behaviour. The style of life is dynamically represented through the idea of *movement* and *teleology*. Implicitly, the style of life runs through the divisible self and both are based on underlying or foundational unity, perhaps soul. Style of life, self and soul are implied 'as-if' they exist. There is no way one can absolutely quantify or measure these ideas. These are philosophical issues that cannot be easily solved. The notion of 'as-if' is a philosophical proposition drawn from the neo-Kantian philosophy of Vaihinger ([1925]1965). Adlerians use Vaihinger's 'as-if' to point to the meaningful implications of ideas that cannot necessarily be objectively validated but are nevertheless powerful subjective forces, 'as-if' they could be objectively known. 'Show me a soul', a sceptic might ask. This no one can do any more than someone can 'show' the unconscious. Adlerians subscribe to a subjectivistic approach to human psychology; propositions that are meaningful forces in human life (though not necessarily for all humans) are taken into account on the basis of 'as-if'.

Vaihinger also influenced Adler with his concept of fictionalism, which the Ansbachers (in Adler 1956: 77) sum up as: 'ideas, including unconscious notions, which have no counterpart in reality which serve the useful function of enabling us to deal with [reality] better than we could otherwise'. In the spirit of Kant, Vaihinger emphasizes the subjectivity of the fiction, which works on the principle of 'as-if'. For example, Adler understands gender (femininity and masculinity) as constructed fictions, 'as-if' such constructions really did exist as fixed, objective reality. Here, Adler implicitly articulates a distinction between sex and gender with associated power dynamics running both ways.

By accepting Vaihinger's fiction as integral to psychic functioning, Adler believes that an individual will construct and rework (often through internalization of available material) their own images, ideas and beliefs (fictions) about phenomena as an artist would give shape to an impression on a canvas. According to Adler, the human psyche is intrinsically creative. By fashioning their fiction, individuals simultaneously create a goal to strive for, and a biased apperception with which to view others and the world in relation to this goal. This *guiding fiction* is based on a schema that leads to a fictional final goal that is ultimately never possible to achieve.

Fictions arise, according to Adler, due to the gendered self emerging in a world where gender dynamics accord hierarchies and internalizations of these hierarchies become conflated with a subjective sense of competency, mastery and sense of lack (inferiority). Adler asserts that all children strive from a felt minus to a felt plus, from inferiority to superiority, through compensations that are based on an individual's appropriation of socially constructed gendered hierarchies. In drawing attention to the social dynamics of sexuality and ascribed roles, Adler was the first to argue a psychoanalytic position in support of feminism (no doubt influenced by his wife Raissa who was a strong feminist) as Kurzweil (1995), Tong (1989) and Connell (1995) suggest. In a rather radical statement for a man of his period, Adler wrote,

> All our institutions, our traditional attitudes, our laws, our morals, our customs, give evidence of the fact that they are determined and maintained by privileged males for the glory of male domination. These institutions reach out into the very nurseries and have a great influence upon the child's soul. A child's understanding of these relationships need not be very great, but we must admit that his emotional life is immensely affected by them.
>
> (Adler 1927: 123)

Adler uses the fictional final goal interchangeably with the *guiding self-ideal* a term he introduced in 1912 just after his break with Freud. This notion, as the Ansbachers (Adler 1956) point out, preceded Freud's first usage of the 'ego ideal' in 1914, a concept that was the forerunner to Freud's superego. The notion of *narcissism* is important for both theorists' understanding of the self's striving for ideals and associated guilt and/or shame. What Adler and Freud shared was an understanding of the self as being deeply influenced by societal and biological differences around sex (male, female) and gender (masculinity, femininity); Freud generally emphasized the former and Adler the latter. (Since Freud did not explicitly speak of the self, our remarks constitute an inferred observation.) In terms of the self as a sexed and gendered subject, it is notable to heed Freud's warning: 'the concepts of "masculine" and "feminine", whose meaning seems so unambiguous to ordinary people, are amongst the most confused that occur in science' ([1905]1953: 219, footnote).

Adler and (dis)unity of the self

Historically, Ansbacher and Ansbacher (Adler 1956: 62) have noted that: 'Adler was one of the voices in the wilderness of pre-World War I days crying that the self or soul must remain the focal point if psychology is to provide satisfactory explanations'. Anglo-American

Adlerians view the self as a fundamental subject of their psychology. Hoffman (1994) titled his biography of Adler *The Drive for Self,* his motive being largely to keep a differentiation with psychoanalysis. This differentiation has been blurred somewhat in contemporary terms as much of psychoanalysis is now generally accepting of the concept of the self (excepting notably the Lacanian school). This is particularly evinced by Kohut's psychoanalytic school of *self psychology* (see Chapter 4). Prior to Kohut, other psychoanalytic theorists who never used an explicit theory of self nevertheless paved the way for followers to make use of their material. Thomas offers a Kleinian example:

> The force of the Kleinian position is that human destructiveness and the potential for fragmentation can only be partially contained; it will be defensively projected out into the world, increasing paranoia and affecting social life and the formation of social structures. The chaos within the self appears in the external world.
>
> (Thomas 1996: 325)

Both psychoanalytic and Adlerian conceptions of self are predicated on unconscious defence and safeguarding strategies. The former is theorized on conflict, the latter on the unity of the style of life. In psychoanalytic object relations, internalized objects (introjected others) may conflict with one another, and in so doing, reveal the multiple nature of the self. Overall, these psychoanalytic views do, however, emphasize conflict more so than the Adlerian position.

Adler's emphasis on the unity of the style of life was deepened through his readings of the holistic philosophy of Smuts who wrote:

> Nowhere in the world do we find a greater intensity of the holistic effect produced than in the individual self or personality. And yet even there it is by no means complete, for the individual personality, as we shall see, still shows a discordance of elements which leads to most of the great problems of thought and conduct.
>
> (Smuts 1973: 246)

In emphasizing holism Adler did not naïvely overlook the occurrence of fractures within the self. He did, however, view such fractures as governed by the underlying unity intrinsic to the style of life: 'With every individual we must look below the surface . . . for the underlying coherence, for the unity [or self-consistency] of the personality' (Adler 1956: 189).

Other self theorists, such as McAdams (1997), underscore the ways in which the self differs internally. He draws attention to the splits between the self ideal, the actual and the undesired self. Each representation can differ markedly, which constitutes possible fracturing of the self and related discords. Adler (1956), too, emphasized a guiding self ideal predicated on the notion of the guiding fiction. Whilst recognizing conflict, Adler felt that underlying such conflict is the style of life, which again offers coherence to such conflict. McAdams, perhaps unknowingly, agrees with Adler, when he writes:

> Regardless of how many different self-schemata, self-aspects, self-exemplars, self-bins, or subselves comprise the loose confederacy of an individual's self, the various members of the confederacy all function in the common service of self-consistency and self-enhancement.
>
> (McAdams 1997: 55)

McAdams goes on to cite William James's notion of the 'I' as a function that brings unity and coherence to the multiple and fragmented self. McAdams refers to this process as 'selfing', which he links to the function of the psychoanalytic ego, but an expanded function that transcends the discrete Freudian ego into something much closer to the synthetic function of the Adlerian style of life. This synthetic function was also independently stressed later by Anna Freud (see Chapter 2). The 'me' is a product generated out of the selfing process of the 'I'. McAdams summarizes:

> The developing self seeks a temporal coherence. If the me keeps changing over the long journey of life, then it may be incumbent upon the I to find or construct some form of life coherence and continuity in order for change to make sense.
>
> (McAdams 1997: 62)

For Adler, it is the style of life that governs the multiple self: 'The style of life commands all forms of expression; the whole commands the parts' (1956: 175). Current intellectual trends of postmodernism/poststructuralism tend to dismiss notions of unity and coherence. Before dismissing Adler on this basis we suggest that his writings on unity be read through the notion of the fiction, unity *as-if* unity, self as-if self.

Social approaches to the psychodynamic self

Adler was the first to explore and develop a comprehensive social theory of the psychodynamic self but he was by no means the only one to do so. Closely approximating his theory of self is the work of Karen Horney and Harry Stack Sullivan. We consider some of their ideas here, together with those put forward by Eric Fromm who shared Adler's sympathy for socialism and feminism.

Karen Horney

Karen Horney (1885–1952) developed a variant school of psycho-analysis that she called *holistic psychoanalysis* in reference to her contention that the self must ultimately be viewed as a unitary system. She emphasized the role that culture exerts in the develop-ment of personality and downplayed the classical driven features outlined by Freud and his contemporaries. She put forward a theory of neurosis that posits *basic anxiety* at the core. Psychodynamically Horney asserted that: 'we may have anxiety without knowing it, but that anxiety may be the determining factor in our lives without our being conscious of it' (1937: 40). For many, selfhood is coloured by an underlying feeling of anxiety.

Horney is considered a 'renegade' inasmuch as she challenged the psychoanalytic establishment, arguing that their representations of female psychology are inaccurate. For example, Horney argued that the experience of childbirth and breastfeeding is best seen as a woman's experience *par excellance* and not as a penile substitution. In positing her disagreements, Horney felt that the classical model of selfhood *implied* by psychoanalysis was distorted by a male-centred world-view (Chodorow 1994). Tong summarizes Horney's deviation and its importance to the subject of the self: 'patriarchal culture creates women as feminine (passive, masochistic, narcissistic) and then con-vinces them that "femininity" – actually a defensive adaptation to male domination – characterises their true selves' (1989: 148). For chal-lenging the established psychoanalytic canon, the psychoanalytic establishment in America consequently disqualified Horney as a train-ing analyst in 1941. Perry (quoted in Evans 1996: 48) cites the official reasons given, that her ideas were apparently 'disturbing the students'.

In addition to Horney's writings on feminine psychology, she outlined a model of self that became considerably popular. This model divides the self into four:

1 the *ideal self*: the standard image of perfection that develops psychodynamically as a result of early experiences from parental indifference. This self is a product of compensation, not just out of indifference but also out of wounding as a result of abuse, neglect, feeling unloved or other aspects of inferiority;
2 the *actual self*: the objective 'me' self and the person who is independent of their own or indeed other person's perceptions of them;
3 the *real self*: the often subjectively known core of the person; but also those unconscious elements that together contain an individual's potential, talents and capacity for being. One's uniqueness and spontaneity are located here, as is the self that one becomes aware of through self-realization. This self was what Horney felt the therapeutic process was all about, with the aim of undoing alienation from the real self, to free it and allow it to work spontaneously and creatively in a person's life.
4 the *despised real self*: the container of all negative self-evaluations, a collection of appraisals around poor self-valuation and the feelings one may carry around such as inadequacy, unworthiness and feeling unlovable. Horney's famous conception of the *tyranny of the 'should'*, that voice which internally criticizes and autocratically demands that one should be *x-y-z*, resides here.

Eric Fromm

Eric Fromm (1900–80), like Adler, was deeply influenced by Marx's philosophy and brought to psychoanalysis a critical gaze that would eventually meld with existential problems around the self and meaning. Unlike Adler, Fromm was more concerted in his contextualizing of the western self as problematic under capitalism. Hence he drew considerable attention, as well as caused controversy for politicizing the self in a discipline that generally steers clear of the right–left political divide. Fromm is strongly associated with the psychoanalytic left, although others have criticized him for eventually compromising his early radicalism by too readily adopting existentialism (Jacoby 1975).

Fromm once noted: 'In the 19th century the problem was that God is dead; in the 20th century the problem is that man is dead' (cited in Monte 1987: 407). How did Fromm arrive at such a startling polemic? He begins by contextualizing the self under the currents of history and by taking this contextualization into two fundamental modes of existence: *having* and *being*. These modes represent two contrasting points of reference for relating to the self, others and the world at large. In the *having* mode, selfhood is predicated on a materialist and consumption oriented *marketing character*, where individuals regard themselves as commodities and find meaning and purpose through the act of acquiring and consuming private property. Fromm writes:

> The statement '*I* [subject] have *O* [object]' expresses a definition of *I* through my possession of *O*. The subject is not *myself* but *I am what I have*. My property constitutes myself and my identity.
>
> (Fromm 1998: 54, Fromm's italics)

Fromm reasoned that an individual caught up in the *having* mode is engaged with the world of 'things' and that such an orientation lacks 'aliveness', it is engagement with 'deadness'. An individual who develops a pathological style of 'having' and therefore a love of that which is dead is referred to as a *necrophile*. Fromm contrasted the *having* mode with the *being* mode. In *being*, he posited an existential condition that emphasizes experiencing in a non-alienated fashion. Fromm (1998: 86) comments: 'In order to acquire a genuine sense of self . . . He has to give up holding on to himself as a thing and begin to experience himself only in the process of creative response'. In *being*, Fromm asserts that human subjects are better able to experience joy, tenderness, and love than under the auspices of *having*. This is because the fear of death that underlies existential anxiety becomes transformed through the *being* mode:

> The fear then, is not of dying, but of *losing what I have*: the fear of losing my body, my ego, my possessions, and my identity; the fear of facing the abyss of nonidentity, of 'being lost' . . . To the extent that we live in the having mode, we must fear dying.
>
> (Fromm 1998: 103–4, original emphasis)

Fromm disputed the metaphysical determinism that was evident in evolutionary psychology. In contrast he asserted that people are historically and culturally sensitive entities subject to unconscious appropriation of prevailing norms and values. While these norms and values might seem natural (such as aggression in a warrior society or cooperation in a farming communal society) Fromm (1998: 121) argued they are largely socially determined. Citing Freud, Spinoza and Nietzsche, he comments: 'most of what is real is not conscious, and most of what we are conscious of is not real, is fiction and cliché'. For Fromm the power of cultural backdrop in shaping human subjects overrides biological determinism. In this line of thinking he strongly echoes Horney (the two were intimate associates) and evinces his departure from the orthodox Freudian drive model.

Finally, Fromm had some interesting things to say about character. The self is unique by virtue of a largely unconscious appropriation of culture, however individualized, in which a 'structure' is formed. This structure apparently changes little over the lifespan but is also not fully immutable. What troubled Fromm was the way capitalism sought to establish a marketing character as the social backdrop appropriated unconsciously by the individual. Such a repressed character is subject to anonymous authoritarianism through *automaton conformity*, an *escape from freedom* predicated on a strategy to avoid anxiety by being the same as everyone else. Repression is the mechanism that shrouds and mystifies the 'truth' of this appropriation. For each culture there is a *social unconscious* that is embedded within the individual. Fromm states: 'We repress not only what is bad, but also what is good, because it does not fit the character of society . . . What we repress the most is the truth, because it is the most dangerous thing for our entire way of living' (1998: 123–4). Through analysis, the individual unmasks the extent to which they have hidden 'the truth', a truth that has its origins in the social world.

Harry Stack Sullivan

Harry Stack Sullivan (1892–1949) also shifted to the social realm, and in so doing made a monumental though frequently overlooked contribution to American psychiatry. His theory is interchangeably known as *interpersonal psychiatry* or *interpersonal psychoanalysis*. Sullivan was notoriously disdainful of both psychoanalysis and psychiatry, and a dissenter within both fields. In the former he retained basic psychoanalytic assumptions such as transference and the unconscious. In the latter he challenged the dominant Kraepelinian model of psychiatry and stressed a holistic, interpersonal approach. Sullivan's fresh ideas attracted some of the brightest figures to his Washington School, an interdisciplinary training institute for psychiatrists, psychologists, social workers, counsellors and clergy. Horney, Fromm, Thompson and Fromm-Reichman were all associates of Sullivan and shared much common philosophical ground. Like the other neo-Freudians that Sullivan worked with, he rejects the orthodox Freudian drive model, although he retains a variant of the pleasure principle by emphasizing the dynamic interplay between euphoria and tension. However, Evans (1996: 15) notes that Sullivan's 'need to separate himself from Freud was perhaps so great that he persistently invented new, often obtuse, terms for concepts already well expressed by Freud'.

Like Adler and the above-mentioned associates of Sullivan, the theory of interpersonal psychoanalysis emphasizes the individual's context as essential to understanding selfhood. Indeed, Sullivan's uncompromising view of the self as interpersonally oriented led Gordon Allport to declare that 'Sullivan, perhaps more than any other person, labored to bring about the fusion of psychiatry and social science' (cited in Evans 1996: 6). In this regard, Sullivan felt that an interdisciplinary approach was required to understand both selfhood and mental health issues. A singular though collective view from within the bounded discipline of psychiatry would necessarily be insufficient. For this reason, the journal *Psychiatry*, which Sullivan co-founded, welcomed contributions from a wide variety of disciplines and theoretical standpoints.

In interpersonal psychoanalysis selfhood is based on the notion of *personifications*. Similar to Adler's *style of life*, personifications embody one's assumptions, schemata, internalized representations of others and reflected appraisals of the self. Personifications develop out of developmental experiences. These modes of experience impact the way the *self-system* develops. The central function of the self-system is to ward off anxiety, to avoid disapproval from others and to impose some coherence on to what might otherwise be a chaotic, perplexing and complex world. How one experiences the social/material world begins in infancy through the *prototaxic* mode where the infant has only a marginalized sense of themselves as separate entities. Later, the infant is able to perceive the past, present and anticipate the future through cognitive maturation. The *parataxic* mode is associated with consequences/anticipations. It is the basis for the later ambiguities in interpersonal relations that Sullivan termed *parataxic distortion*. In this phenomenon, the self-system shrouds or otherwise distorts experiences in ways that seek the avoidance of anxiety. A common expression of this distortion is evinced when individuals come to unconsciously relate to people as if they were others, or based on past experiences with others. It is a very similar concept to the standard psychoanalytic transference/projection mechanisms.

Sullivan was not unique in insisting that one's personal stereo-types and prejudices may carry dire social consequences. Indeed, this was the thrust of the Frankfurt School's much cited research on the *authoritarian personality* (Adorno *et al.* 1950). In the same spirit as those working with Adorno at the Frankfurt School, Sullivan wrote on the negative effects of racism, anti-Semitism and other issues relevant to the field of political psychology. Indeed, he published a highly provocative paper titled *The Illusion of Personal Individuality* that sought to articulate the problems of viewing the individual as an isolated a priori entity (Sullivan 1950). For Sullivan, all our actions carry interpersonal consequences that have ramifications on the personal and mental health levels. For this and other reasons, Sullivan worked actively in the World Health Organization as a means for promoting cultural harmony and mental health. Evans cites Sullivan's epitaph (which Sullivan wrote himself) where he urged his colleagues to use their academic and clinical skills to promote a world based on 'enduring peace and social progress' (1996: 51).

Summary

In this chapter we have outlined the central contributors of the social approach to the psychodynamic self. Consistent with the traditions of these schools, current theorists of the social and psychodynamic self are working in the spaces between social and political theory and psychoanalysis (Wolfenstein 1993; Chodorow 1994; Hinshelwood 1996). These approaches stress the interpersonal aspects of relating in the context of one's group, culture and society. A consistent critique levelled at most theorists cited above is that they compromise the intrapersonal interiority of the psyche. Specifi-cally, they are criticized for focusing too much on the role of society and culture at the expense of deep unconscious phenomena such as phantasy and biologically based/mediated psychic conflict. Never-theless, they have contributed an enduring and vital collection of standpoints relating to the human subject that has become central to twentieth-century conceptions of the self and personality and related clinical practices.

CHAPTER 6

Jungian and post-Jungian perspectives on the psychodynamic self

The Swiss psychiatrist Carl Gustav Jung (1875–1961) was, like Adler before him, an associate of Freud and supporter of psychoanalysis. Indeed, he was the first in his field to apply psychoanalytic ideas to the treatment of schizophrenia. Also like Adler, Jung would come to disagree and subsequently break with Freud after a collaboration lasting several years. Notoriously, this was a very difficult break. Freud had planned for Jung to succeed to the top of the psychoanalytic movement, to carry forward the torch of psychoanalysis, and it was a great disappointment when Jung made clear his dissension and departed. There were complex dynamics between Freud and Jung that contributed to their rift. The nature of the libido was a principal point of intellectual disagreement but by no means the only one. The details that lead to their break-up are poignantly documented in their published correspondence (see: *The Freud/Jung Letters*, McGuire 1974).

After his break with Freud, Jung founded his own school of depth psychology, which he referred to as *analytical psychology*. Analytical psychology explicitly places great emphasis on the self. Whereas Freud implicitly referred to self, Jung explicitly stressed the self within his divergent theory. Indeed, the Self as archetype in analytical psychology is amongst this school's most exalted and pre-eminent concepts. The capitalization of the Self in archetypal theory is meant to distinguish the archetype from normal linguistic references to (the lower-case) self. What follows is a brief summary of Jung's model of personality and depth psychology and then a discussion of the Self. We have included post-Jungian comments where warranted in recognition that analytical psychology, like psychoanalysis, has variegated and diversified since Jung's death.

Basic structure of the psyche

Jung emphasized a general psychic energy, *libido*, that was not fundamentally driven by erotic and sexual impulses, though it could certainly include such impulses. Jung's libido, as Beebe (1989: 9) notes, is not just energy but *purposeful* energy. More generally, this psychic energy represents the need for wholeness and *individuation*, that is a drawing together of parts split off, asunder or otherwise disparate. The concept is linked though not identical to Schopenhauer's conception of will (*principus individuationis*). Beebe says individuation 'has come to mean the will of the psychological individual to become conscious' (1998: 58). The push toward consciousness is undoubtedly a central configuration in Jung's model of personality. This push is also influenced by the style in which an individual seeks experiences; the *extroverted* person seeks stimulation more from external events while the *introverted* person seeks stimulation from internal ones.

Jung was very much influenced both by James's notion of the self and by the Protestantism in which he was raised (his father was a clergyman). He was keenly interested in all varieties of symbolism and derived many of his ideas from the symbols his patients reported to him as well as from his own dreams. Jung's personal struggle with, and interest in Christianity both colour and pervade his collected works. However, he also derived many of his ideas from other religious traditions such as Bhuddism, Taoism and pagan mythologies. Medieval practices such as alchemy also figure in his model of the human psyche; he saw the alchemist's desire to change base matter into gold as a complex metaphor for psychic integration and wholeness.

In describing individuation as a life-long quest, Jung relies on a teleological conception of wholeness and completeness that includes the psychic need for meaning. The notion of a higher power, to the chagrin of many in more strictly materialist corners of psychology, is central to much of Jungian thinking. Storr notes, 'whereas Nietzsche stated that God was dead, Jung rediscovered God as a guiding principle of unity within the depths of the individual psyche' (1983: 25). The individual psyche itself is made up of an indeterminate number of *complexes*, which are clusters of psychic associations with their own autonomous tension. Jung referred to them as 'partial or fragmentary personalities' (Jung cited in Storr 1983: 82). When stimulated these 'personalities' can cause an individual to experience somatic reactions (shortness of breath, neurotic pain and so on). Complexes, being semi-autonomous, point to Jung's conception of the psyche as fragmented and largely unconscious. At the centre of consciousness lies the *ego* that Jung saw as 'a bit of consciousness which floats upon the ocean of dark things' (1968: 21). Samuels points out that Jung's conception of ego as an 'entity . . . responsible for identity and personal continuity in time and space' (1985: 56). The ego entity is itself a complex that functions 'in the service of something greater than itself' (1985: 58) for example, the Self. The ego is a conscious function which serves the Self in a peculiar way: 'the ego must try to dominate the psyche and the self must try to make the ego give up that attempt' (1985: 58).

Ultimately the ego is subordinate to the vastly larger and deeper parts of the psyche that include: (1) the *personal unconscious* and (2) the *collective unconscious*. Jung offers his fundamental distinction: 'Whereas the contents of the personal unconscious are acquired during the individual's lifetime, the contents of the collective unconscious are invariably archetypes that were present from the beginning' (CW 9, para. 13).[6] The notion of unconsciousness was certainly not unique to Jung, Freud or Adler. However, these three made use of the concept in innovative ways that helped to cast light onto the nature of the human subject. Light itself is a metaphor intrinsic to the conscious/unconscious dyad. Samuels notes: 'When ego-consciousness illuminates something, what is on the periphery is in darkness' (1985: 65).

Within the personal unconscious lie the contents of forgotten experiences, usually available for recall and particular to the individual, hence personal. However, the deeper one travels down into the personal unconscious, Jungians argue, the nearer one comes to the sediment of universal, eternal images that Jung refers to as *archetypes*. We will have more to say about some of these images shortly. The archetypes are found within the collective unconscious. This notion of a 'collective unconscious' is difficult to define. Jung is referring to a layer of unconsciousness that he asserts is common to all persons regardless of race, culture and so on. Jung argues that our own personal experience of the collective unconscious is generally through the mechanisms of transference/projection. Jung states:

> The contents of the *collective unconscious* are not subject to any arbitrary intention and are not controllable by the will. They

actually behave as if they did not exist within yourself – you see them in your neighbours but not in yourself.

(Jung 1968: 50)

The thrust of this structuring of the psyche suggests that we are under many 'influences' beyond our individual control. Indeed, he goes on to explicitly state: 'We are not really masters in our house' (Jung 1968: 81). Jung attempted to prove his theory through analysis of the autarchic symbol-producing potential of the collective unconscious. For example, he analysed the psychotic productions of schizophrenics as one of many sources to confirm his theory.

Archetypal theory

Jung borrowed the term *archetype* from an expression used by St Augustine. There are many readings of what Jung meant by the term. For simplicity we shall quote Jung's own definition, summarized at one of his famous Tavistock lectures held in London during the autumn of 1935: 'An archetype means a typos [imprint], a definite grouping of archaic character containing, in form as well as in meaning, *mythological motifs*' (Jung 1968: 41). Archetypes may appear in fairy tales, legends, folklore, dreams, as well as in the hallucinations and fantasies of psychotic episodes. Archetypes may also be represented in literature, poetry, painting, sculpture and other forms of creative expression. Archetypes move unconsciously in ways that organize experience. Much of this influence pervades the psyche through the production of imagery or corresponding events in the outer world such as in the meaningful coincidences Jung called *synchronicity*. Synchronous events suggest that archetypes stand outside of space and time and factor meaningful coincidences to occur so as to externalize an inner event.

Jungians generally believe that there are an indeterminate number of archetypes. Three archetypal constellations will be considered here: (1) *Persona*, (2) *shadow* and (3) *anima/animus*. This little sketch of each serves only as a brief example and is of necessity insufficient. In a survey book such as this space limitations prevent a proper analysis of the many central archetypes that Jungians generally configure as influencing psychic life. Our examination also partly sidesteps the controversy surrounding archetypal theory within the post-Jungian schools. For example Tacey finds that many archetypal readings 'sound remarkably like social stereotypes' (1997: 18) that, in the case of the gendered anima/animus, 'produce a new Jungian fundamentalism' (Tacey 1997: 32). One of the issues that post-Jungian thinkers such as Hillman (1983), Samuels (1985), Tacey (1997) and Kulkarni (1997) examine and criticize is the notion of fixed, never changing, deterministic archetypes that somehow order and integrate psychic life. Samuels proposes that: 'Present-day Jungian analysts, especially those touched by postmodernism and its eschewing of meta-narratives, are far less convinced that universal and eternal images [archetypes] exist' (1998: 24).

Jung's suggestion, that we are not 'master's in our house', opens up the gates of 'fate', which ostensibly takes away aspects of an individual's free will. This conception of human nature motivates some critical challenges to Jung's central ideas, many by his own contemporary adherents. Could this be the reason why some post-Jungians, such as Hillman, have cast out Jung's religious theology, emphasis on unity, teleology, as well as his reliance on metaphysics? If so, it has not discouraged such thinkers from innovating new approaches, broadening the value bases of analytical psychology and therefore opening up to those who otherwise might have stayed away. In this sense diversification seems to be an integral aspect of the post-Jungian movement.

In disputing aspects of Jungian thinking, post-Jungians have moved beyond Jung in differing ways. Samuels (1985) coined the term *post-Jungian* by which he referred to those connected yet also distant from Jung. Kulkarni elaborates: 'a post-Jungian is someone who acknowledges a debt to Jung, but refuses to be bound by Jung's particular and limited vision' (1998: 98). These differences with classical Jungian theory are complex and affect the meaning and configuration of so many central ideas in Jungian theory as to pose no further unity on fundamental matters such as the meaning and function of archetypes. In this regard, the controversy that post-Jungian ideas provoke is stimulating, but also self-critical. Samuels (1998) asks in a recent chapter heading, 'Will the post-Jungians survive?' Samuels identifies four major Jungian schools: (1) fundamentalist, (2) classical, (3) developmental and (4) psychoanalytic. Each school has its own perspective on the issues brought up in this chapter.

The Persona

The archetype of the Persona has been posed by Jung as a complex entity that separates the public person from the private. It is a concept Jungians have used metaphorically by reference to the Greek *mask*. This mask, Persona, has ties to social and public identity. It serves to obscure and hide the inner nature of the Self. Jung constructed this archetype by reference to the practices of his time, that people generally had rather fixed roles in society, for example, holding a single career for the duration of their working lives. In taking on the public identity of a cobbler, one would also construct an 'artificial' personality in keeping with public expectations of this role. It would be incumbent on cobblers to behave in a cobbler-like manner.

In adopting an artificial personality, ostensibly, the person would have to pay for this inauthenticity by compensatory means. Jung says: 'A man cannot get rid of himself in favour of an artificial personality without punishment' (CW 7, para. 307). The Persona is subsequently implicated for a catalogue of symptoms such as compulsive disorders, phobias, shifting moods, vices and so on. Why is this the case? Jung saw the Persona as making too many concessions to external life at the expense of internal life. He saw the ego as being one-sidedly occupied, indeed, overly identified with the Persona. This one-sidedness purportedly incites compensatory reactions with other archetypes, such as the anima.

Over the past century there have been great shifts in the way those of us in the West spend our public lives. Many of us have or will have dual or even triple careers, changing hats several times during our working lives. The boundaries between private and public have blurred so while women breast feed in their offices, men now finish reports on the ironing board or email their web servers during the laundry's spin cycle. Although proposed as problematic, concepts like the Persona are nevertheless useful. Corresponding concepts proliferate across the psychotherapies, though without the archetypal underpinnings. The next section examines the anima/animus. The anima in particular is posed as the opposite of Persona suggesting that many of Jung's archetypes are intimately linked with one another.

Anima/animus

One of the means by which the psyche strives towards individuation is through a complex constellation of opposites. The emergence of opposites as part of the psyche's unconscious quest for holism, based on compensation, is a process Jung referred to as *enantiodromia*. In psychic development, a one-sided emphasis pulls forward its unconscious opposite. A central example of this tendency is found in Jung's conceptions around contrasexuality. In analytical psychology, the masculine archetype *animus* and the feminine archetype *anima* are construed as such opposites. The Persona of women is said to configure an unconscious animus and, as we saw above, in men an unconscious anima. The Latin term anima actually refers to the soul whilst animus to the intellect. Both terms are representative of the broad based principles that Jung referred to as *Eros* and *Logos*. Eros is said to represent the feminine principle of love and relatedness whilst Logos points to rationality and logic. Young-Eisendrath (1998) has analysed the anima and animus as represented in Jungian writings, concluding that Jung based these archetypes on biological as well as cultural splitting of male/female and masculine/feminine. In using these binary distinctions, Jung made transparent the effect that nineteenth-century divisions between culture (masculinity) and nature (femininity) had on his own thinking.

Post-Jungians such as Kulkarni (1997) have deconstructed Jung's ideas on contrasexuality, concluding that Jung's ideas are inherently biased, indeed tainted through (hetero) sexism. Young-Eisendrath (1998) posits that Jung, like all depth psychologists of his time, produced ideas and concepts that were replete with 'androcentric' biases. What constitutes the 'feminine'? Do archetypes cause men to be externally strong and internally weak? Does this apply to all men? Are feminine women weak or is femininity constituted by weakness? By placing the anima, or feminine soul, as opposite the public persona, it appears that Jung simply sided with the stereotypes of his own and earlier times. The following quote illustrates:

> The persona, the ideal picture of a man as he should be, is inwardly compensated by feminine weakness, and as the individual outwardly plays the strong man, so he becomes inwardly a woman, i.e., the anima, for it is the anima that reacts to the persona.
>
> (CW 7, para. 309)

Andrew Samuels questions the traditional Jungian emphasis on gender certainty, suggesting that in fact the psyche is quite often engaged in gender uncertainty. Recognizing that the differences in morphology between the sexes ought not be trivialized, Samuels nevertheless concludes that the old anima/animus – Eros/Logos divisions are beyond redemption: 'the argument that innate psychological differences between the sexes are based on the body has serious and insidious difficulties in it' (1989: 101). Drawing on Lacanian and Kleinian perspectives, the post-Jungian Young-Eisendrath argues that the notion of 'Otherness' based on unconscious fantasies fuelled by fear, envy, jealousy and hatred is what the complexes of the anima and animus are based on. For her, this 'dialectic of desire' has more to do with the dangers of dividing the human community into discrete opposites than with the supposedly intrinsic, fixed and metaphysical images of anima/animus. For this reason, she has disposed of the Latin terms anima/animus altogether, whilst retaining, in the new post-Jungian tradition, a claim to being a Jungian nevertheless.

If nothing else, the archetypes of the anima and animus seem to point to the significance that sex and gender hold for the psyche. Cognitive psychologists posit gender identity as core to one's self-schemata. The belief that we are masculine or feminine and what that means to us personally as well as socially is bound to have some effect on our inner lives. During late modernity, the period in which Jung lived, gender roles were very strictly construed, with little public tolerance for deviation. Perhaps the idea of an unconscious masculinity in women and an unconscious femininity in men was suitable psychic fodder for that period. It is quite feasible that this is less so now. Nevertheless, Beebe's comments on the role of the anima in men sum up nicely the reasons why contrasexuality becomes such a popular element of Jungian thinking:

> The anima was Jung's central discovery in the field of masculine psychology, for, as he learned, only the anima can deliver a man into a consciousness that is based, not on heroic self-mastery, but rather on empathic participation in life.
>
> (Beebe 1989: xi)

Hence, the appeal to so many frustrated individuals who undoubtedly found the pursuit of a limiting 'masculine' consciousness one-sidedly unsuitable, even dangerous for self-evolution.

The Shadow

The Shadow is a nebulous archetype to discuss; any attempt to cast light onto darkness cancels the latter out and blinds one from seeing 'it'. With this difficulty in mind, Jung saw the Shadow as operating through transference and projection. Shadow figures might include scapegoats such as 'criminals', illicit drug users, the poor, the diseased, the sexually different or any other group/individual who may be easy targets upon which our repressed, hence dark impulses might be projected. For example, the Nazis were actively engaged in creating propaganda that would encourage the masses to view Jews, Gypsies, homosexuals and other groups as suitable screens onto which feelings of hatred and rage might be projected. The exercise is largely an irrational one. Think yourself if you have perhaps met and instantly disliked someone, but for no apparent reason. Jungians suggest that such an individual may have triggered your shadow by openly displaying attributes of which you yourself may be unconscious, thus your uncomfortableness with it. What irritates or constellates dislike for you is maybe not the other, but a facet of yourself projected.

There is a strong moral element to the Shadow. When those re-pressed and unacceptable features of our own personalities are thrown out of oneself and onto others, invoking strong feelings, fear, loath-ing and hatred, we experience a sense of dissociation: Not me but that. Samuels suggests that the Shadow's integration 'is vital if man is to develop . . . he must see that *he* is the problem. It is not a question of getting rid of the Shadow, but recognising it and integ-rating it' (1985: 66). Beebe takes this to heart when, he proclaims, in his analysis of the moral idea of character, that the Shadow will diminish as individuation proceeds: 'individuation, which is deeply rooted in alchemical imagery and fantasy, encourages the expecta-tion of a dissolving of the Shadow traits of character as development proceeds to maturity' (1998: 53). Thus, the end point of the Shadow is its integration so that darkness is replaced with the light of consciousness.

The Self as archetype

Philosophically, Jung's tradition radiates out of German idealism and associated Romanticism. These traditions suggest that who and what we are is essentially beyond the telling. For Jung, the fabric of being is a life-long quest of becoming gradually more conscious of forces beyond one's control, deep in the unconscious where 'the dragon of chaos lives' (Jung 1968: 137). Jung summarizes his idea on the Self in relation to the ego:

The ego stands to the self as the moved to the mover, or as object to subject, because the determining factors which radiate out from the self surround the ego on all sides and are therefore supraordinate to it. The self, like the unconscious, is an a priori existent out of which the ego evolves.

(CW 11, para. 391)

The Self's goal of individuation is a quest for 'totality' brought about through periodic descents into the unconscious, a place where therapy or analysis could facilitate the individual's quest for holism. Jung draws our attention to the meaning of holism, the goal of individuation: 'to make holy or to heal' (1968: 137). The most common symbol of this journey to wholeness is drawn from the Sanskrit word *mandala*, which means circle. Mandalas could be sketched, painted or represented through other imagery as appearing in dreams or in psychotic hallucinations. Jung spent many a late evening drawing these symbols of the Self to which he noticed a peculiar healing ability, their appearance coinciding with deep meaning for the individuation process.

Fordham notes that Jung derived his understanding of the Self largely from eastern mysticism, that it is a concept shrouded in mysticism which Jung states is 'beyond proof, beyond science' (Fordham 1985: 25). In potential contradiction, Fordham (1985: 16) also notes that the Self is objective and independent of the subjective realm, he again cites Jung: 'As for the self it is completely outside the personal sphere'. In this vein, Fordham declares the Self a psychic reality, a 'fact'. In developing his ideas on the Self, Fordham turned to the developmental pathology of autism. He also pays attention to the psychic lives of children and adolescents to which he faults Jung and most Jungians for almost entirely ignoring. Moreover, Fordham disputes the conventional wisdom of Jungians around paying too much attention to the second half of life (from middle age onwards) declaring that 'the same self can be recognized in childhood and that its actions underlie infantile experience from birth onwards' (1985: xi).

As a psychic function, the Self is said to be an archetype of order, one that draws together one's split-off parts, it therefore has an integrative function. The Self, as an independent configuration, is also *transpersonal*. Moreover, it can also be a destructive force; Fordham has observed how Self can also act to *deintegrate*. As a source of psychic distress, Samuels notes the role of the Self in psychopathology. He argues that the Self often 'manifests as a defensive concern with hierarchy, logic, precision, definition, structure, pattern, regularity, and order at the expense of reversibility, mobility, and interaction' (1989: 12). He goes on to cite Guggenbühl-Craig, who warns of the danger of succumbing to the 'cult of the complete, healthy and round, [person who aspires] to mandala-like perfection' (1989: 223). For Samuels, Self worship towards an idealized state of perfection is itself deeply problematic. Perhaps this is why, in the beginning of his text *The Plural Psyche*, Samuels cites Winnicott's warning: 'we are poor indeed if we are only sane' (1989: 5).

Jung's spirituality is evidenced most clearly in the archetype of the Self. There is no denying Jung's metaphysical bent when analysing this concept; for him it includes the *numinous* or a sense of sublime harmony. He states that 'Christ is our nearest analogy of self and its meaning' (CW 9ii, para. 79). In the final analysis, it seems that the Jungian notion of Self goes well beyond science and ends up more as an article of faith (though Fordham clearly rejects this claim – see his book *The Objective Psyche*, 1958). If the archetype of Self exists on the basis of faith, this certainly need not distress most, even those who are agnostic or atheist. Indeed, faith in the unknown can be much more than faith in an established religion or religious figure. Because a cure for cancer does not currently exist does not prevent one from having faith in the possibility. In regard to the Self, this seems to be Jung's own conclusion for he states:

> By 'self' we mean psychic wholeness, but what realities under-lie this concept we do not know, because psychic contents cannot be observed in their unconscious state, and moreover the psyche cannot know itself.
>
> (CW 10, para. 779)

Summary

The Self is the central archetype in analytical psychology and has been the basis of much discussion amongst both traditional and post-Jungians alike. As an archetype that serves at least in part an integrative function, it brings together all the disparate parts of the personality towards the goal of individuation. We have considered some of these parts such as the Persona, the shadow and the anima/animus. We have also considered some of the disagreements Jungians have engaged with around these issues. We wish to emphasize the vastness of these discussions, indeed entire books have been written on the Self archetype alone.

The next chapter looks at cognitive approaches to the self. Whereas Jungian approaches are grounded in nineteenth-century Romanticism or re-read through postmodernity, the cognitive perspectives are rooted more in the functionalism that comes out of modernity. These differences in philosophical grounding will become clear as we proceed.

CHAPTER 7

Cognitive perspectives on the self

The cognitive school has emerged on the psychology stage as a distinct subject domain over the past 30–40 years, gaining strength and momentum very early in its ascendancy. During this time it has established a considerable body of knowledge and associated practice. Though newer than psychoanalysis and behaviourism it is nevertheless rooted in earlier ideas in philosophy and psychology.

Cognitive psychology has only recently considered the self in any detail, and originally did not consider it at all. This school, particularly the area of cognitive therapy, is a somewhat newer field of interest within psychology. Its major achievement was to unseat behaviourism as one of the dominant forces in academic psychology, through the so called 'cognitive revolution' of the 1960s. This is somewhat inaccurate, even a myth, because many psychologists interested in cognitive psychology did not overthrow behaviourism. Rather, they retained their interest in behaviourism, melding the two together in the overlapping domain of cognitive-behavioural psychology. Therefore the 'cognitive revolution' was hardly a revolution, but more of a marriage; however, many identify as 'cognitive' only and eschew the hyphen with behaviourism. Most 'cognitive-only' psychologists nevertheless wholeheartedly adopted or retained behaviourism's core epistemology (views on how to produce knowledge) and methods (empirical tools). It is also true that 'pure behaviourism' as an area of interest has significantly declined over the past few decades, while similarly a corresponding increase of interest in cognitive psychology has occurred, especially in North America.

Behaviourism had a longstanding policy of ignoring the self. Concerned with objective notions of behaviour, it found the very notion of 'cognitions' problematic, let alone that of the self. Initially, cognitive psychology also precluded the self, preferring staid and operational constructs such as 'schemata' and 'information processing models' without the need for the self-concept to network these ideas together. However, cognitive psychology's failure to acknowledge the self was short-lived. Slowly but certainly, cognitive psychology began to make reference to the self and, starting in the late 1970s, articles specific to the self concept emerged. It was as if an important artefact had surfaced, long forgotten but recognized as precious and integral now that it had been recovered. Indeed, the cognitive psychologist Mahoney (1990: 229) declared that the self is 'the single most important (re)discovery of twentieth-century psychology'.

In reclaiming the self, cognitive psychology also began a project of representing itself as 'interdisciplinary' (Klein 1990). This is evidenced by the boundary-spanning and hyphenating as we earlier pointed out, with the emerging discipline of cognitive-behavioural psychology. It also is evidenced in the making of links with other sub-disciplines in psychology (e.g. developmental psychology), as well as forging links with disciplines such as neuro-psychiatry and linguistics. The cognitive component now has branched beyond, but frequently includes, the broader fields of psychology, linguistics and philosophy, sometimes grouped together under the rubric of *cognitive science*. Cognitive science is undoubtedly a pre-eminent domain within psychology and beyond as an interdisciplinary field that engages several disciplines.

In this chapter we consider some of the research that has emerged from cognitive psychology in regard to the self. We also take a cursory look at Rational Emotive Behaviour Therapy (REBT), not so much for its therapeutic contributions but for its theoretical distinctions from cognitive psychology, that also have implications for the self and personality.

The cognitive perspective: general considerations

The cognitive view of self emphasizes various mental attributes and functions of selfhood such as beliefs, attitudes, perception, memory, language, creative problem solving, reasoning and the ways in which these realms are interrelated. As such, the idea of the self as an area of research and interest in cognitive psychology focuses on the mental representation of selfhood: *self-representation*.

There are several central ideas relevant to the cognitive view of self and personality. The first of these is the notion of *schema* or *schemata*, cognitive structures that constitute one's assumptions, beliefs and biases. The self is organized and populated by schemata. Cognitive psychologists have identified schemata that refer specifically to the self. Sternberg (1999: 164) defines *self-schemata* as 'a very elaborate . . . organised system of internal cues regarding ourselves, our attributes, and our personal experiences'. These schemata point to the fact that human beings are thinking entities who process information. As a species, we are also somewhat self-centred. Sternberg cites research that shows we are more readily able to process information that pertains to ourselves rather than other topics. This view, however, fails to account for the impact of culture in influencing self-schemata. As we saw in Chapter 1, in the comparisons between Americans and Japanese, self-valuation is strongly influenced by culture. This fact is generally overlooked by cognitive psychology.

Beck and Weishaar point out that schemata may be either adaptive or dysfunctional. As the bedrock of personality, schemata 'are enduring cognitive structures, latent during nonstressful periods, that become active when triggered by specific stimuli, stressors, or circumstances' (1989: 293).

The etymology of the word *schema* is rooted in the Greek term meaning a *structure* or *plan*. Thus in cognitive psychology the implications are of mental structures that are based on experience and the various biases implicit in the subjective dimension. Memory is of central personal importance because it influences the ways in which one organizes, assimilates, encodes (and forgets) the specifics of experience. By invoking experience, cognitive psychology points back to Descartes and Locke, the *tabula rasa* (blank slate), and a view of personality influenced by the empiricism of the Enlightenment. Indeed, cognitive psychologists such as Beck and Weishaar (1989) endorse environmental and empirical *social learning theory* as quite compatible with a cognitive standpoint. This places the view of self and personality advanced by cognitivists at odds with more evolutionary or genetic explanations (e.g. Kimura 1999). Biological explanations rely less on experience (environment) and more on heredity-based endowment. While most cognitive psychologists accept genetic influences on personality, they are less bio-deterministic than their colleagues in the fields of bio-psychology and socio-biology. In these fields the focus is on the impact of genes, hormones and other biological stratum in the construction of personality. Bio-psychology and socio-biology have virtually nothing to say about the self.

Self-schemas are specific mental edifices with which we psychologically construct ourselves. At the core of one's self-schemas we generally find structures such as 'gender' (our beliefs that we are male or
female and what this generally means to us). Other issues pertaining
to self-schemas are the specific things we remember about ourselves.
This usually includes our cultural heritage, professional identity,
significant religious and/or political feelings, talents, interests, self-
appraisals and so on.

Schema theory in cognitive psychology is tied to theories of *levels
of processing* in memory research. The idea of processing information
is central to cognitive theory. Describing cognitive therapy, the clinical expression of cognitive psychology, Beck and Weishaar argue that:

> Cognitive therapy is based on a theory of personality which
> maintains that how one thinks largely determines how one
> feels and behaves ... The theory is based on the conception
> that the processing of information is crucial for the survival of
> any organism.
>
> (Beck and Weishaar 1989: 285)

In cognitive psychology, self-schemas are enmeshed with the
construction of identity. In this construction it is the centrality of
memory that makes the identity of the self coherent over time.
Imagine for a moment trying to retain a sense of self in the absence
of any memory whatsoever (long- and short-term). How could it be
possible? Who would we be? How indeed would we be? In cognitive
psychology, the tendency is to focus on specific mental or psychological functions, often to the exclusion of other more holistic functions. The result is an incredible amount of data generated on memory
as a process, yet very little on how memory serves integrative or
holistic aspects of the self.

The second broad issue relevant to the cognitive view of self is the
fact that human experience is shaped by various *biases*. Cognitive
therapy in particular accepts many aspects of *phenomenology*, the
branch of philosophy that focuses on subjective experience. From
this perspective the self is both unique and prone to various pitfalls
such as mis-interpretation and other cognitive errors. For example,
Beck (1967) draws attention to the perennial problem of errors in
reasoning (cognitive distortions), selective abstraction (taking things
out of context), overgeneralizations, magnification and minimization
(catastrophizing or underplaying serious implications), personalization
(usually without evidence of a causal connection) and dichotomous

thinking (thinking in extremes such as 'all or nothing'). In cognitive therapy, symptoms such as depression and anxiety are combated by favourably reworking biased and negative beliefs that we hold in regard to ourselves. This is achieved by focusing on those errors in reasoning that are this mode of therapy's foundation stones, their primary means of focus.

Whereas the behaviourists view human beings as passive respondents to stimuli, the cognitive view emphasizes an active standpoint. For example, memory is not seen as a passive act of storage but rather an active process that involves synthesis.

Cognitive research on the self

Susan Harter and her colleagues are known for their significant contributions to the study of the self in cognitive psychology. Harter's cognitive-developmental work on self-representation puts forward an interesting series of observations and related theorizing. She defines self-representations as 'essential mediators (i.e. to perform a functional role)' (Harter 1990: 116). Reductive causality is used to define these constructs: 'self-related cognitions [are] causal influences on other affective, motivational, or behavioural systems' (1990: 116). Beck and Weishaar (1989: 295) are opposed to characterizing cognitive therapy (as opposed to cognitive psychology) as 'reductive', arguing that 'psychological distress is ultimately caused by many innate, biological, developmental, and environmental factors interacting with one another and so there is no single "cause" of psychopathology'. Moreover, they argue that the cognitive view of personality must not be construed as a 'reductionistic model' but 'recognises that psychological distress is usually the result of many interacting factors' (1989: 295). Similarly Harter argues that self-representations are *multiple* and that 'some [self-representations] emphasise rather specific self-evaluations, others emphasise more global assessments of self-esteem or self-efficacy, whereas others focus on attributions' (Harter 1990: 116).

On a developmental level, Harter both supports and builds on Damon and Hart's (1988) observations on the self as it develops from infancy onwards. Harter (1996) and her colleagues have conducted extensive research to support their conclusions. In particular, she reminds us of the importance of both Cooleys and Mead's *looking-glass self* (Cooley [1902]1922; Mead 1934; see Chapter 1). A cognitive perspective on self-development considers the ability to adopt or imagine the perspectives that others take, the 'looking glass'. Harter writes, 'the very ability to observe, evaluate, praise, and criticize the self must develop through a series of stages that begin with an awareness that *others* are observing, evaluating, praising and criticizing the self' (1990: 122, original emphasis). There are some phenomenological difficulties enmeshed with this process. Young children easily mix up their own wishes and desires with reality. Their narcissistic mixing of fantasy with reality makes their self-statements representative of an 'unreflective litany of desirable talents rather than a serious evaluation of one's attributes' (Harter 1990: 131). This deficit extends to self-valuation reports that fluctuate and are generally unreliable in this flippancy and conflation of reality with fantasy.

It is not until middle to late childhood that children are fully able to compare themselves through their relations with others. It is then that interpersonal dynamics begin to play a greater and conscious role in shaping the child's self-understanding. This also is where one's self becomes integrated with normative expectations. The child's self learns to conform to group norms and to comply with community values through the developmental process.

In early adolescence peer pressure begins to exert even more influence on self-understanding. By middle adolescence, contradictory aspects of the self become more self-evident and potentially distressing. There are 'multiple domains' of self-understanding in relation to others that one is now cognizant of, sometimes acutely so. In Harter's 'lifespan' approach, there are three childhood self-domains; these cluster around: (1) competence, (2) behavioural conduct and (3) social acceptance. By adulthood these domains increase from three to 11, which Harter has identified as: 'intelligence, job competence, athletic competence, sense of humour, morality, sociability, physical appearance, intimate relationships, nurturance, household management, and adequacy as a provider' (1990: 124).

It is during the period of adolescence that the multiplicity of relationships are revealed in greatest complexity in relation to the self. It becomes possible to describe, for example, 'the self with father, mother, close friends, romantic partners, classmates, as well as the self in the role of student, employee, and athlete' (Harter 1990: 124). These selves can diverge one from the other in terms of valuation, satisfaction and integration. Harter's research reveals that the multiple views of self that emerge at this time are more contradictory for girls than boys. For both sexes, however, the complexity of these multiple selves can be the source of great distress. There is greater confusion during this developmental period, which may lead to some self-distortions. This is a period where adolescents make 'the dramatic shift toward introspection, where one takes the self as an object of intense observation and reflection' (Harter 1990: 134). It is here interestingly that Harter draws attention to the psychoanalytic work of Winnicott and his concept of the *false self*, and its associated narcissism and feelings of alienation.

Some parallels with psychoanalytic work are apparent in cognitive psychology. For example, Kihlstrom's (1992) analysis of the cognitive unconscious as a process in metacognition has implications for the cognitive view of self; that is, that there are aspects of it that exist outside of conscious awareness. Other cognitive theorists go even further by integrating core aspects of cognitive theory with psychoanalytic theory. The British cognitive-psychodynamic school founded by Anthony Ryle (1990), known as *Cognitive Analytic Therapy* (CAT), is at present the only such amalgamation known to us.

Rational Emotive Behaviour Therapy (REBT)

Albert Ellis, the founder of REBT, might disagree with our placement of his ideas within a 'cognitive' chapter. Ellis (1980) has long taken great pains to distinguish his school of personality and therapy from the cognitive, cognitive-behavioural and behaviourist schools. However, Ellis acknowledges several areas of overlap between all of these schools. We would have been even more remiss if we had placed REBT in one of the previous psychoanalytic chapters. We believe that we create a lesser error by summarizing his contributions here. Indeed, Beck and Weishaar credit Ellis with influencing cognitive approaches to therapy:

> The work of Albert Ellis gave major impetus to the development of cognitive-behaviour therapies. Both Ellis and Beck believed that people can consciously adopt reason, and both view the patient's underlying assumptions as targets of intervention.
>
> (Beck and Weishaar 1989: 290)

Ellis developed REBT out of his frustration with classical psychoanalysis and other psychodynamic approaches. Nevertheless, some central ideas from both Karen Horney's neo-Freudian school and Alfred Adler's individual psychology became the initial building blocks for REBT, particularly Horney's *tyranny of the shoulds*. Ellis has long been an advocate of Adlerian psychology but prefers Adler's cognitive views over his psychodynamic and social theories. Ellis writes:

> the modern psychotherapist who was the main precursor to REBT was Alfred Adler . . . Adler's motto was *omnia ex opinione suspensa sunt* [everything depends on one's opinion]. It would be hard to state one of the essential tenets of REBT more succinctly and accurately.
>
> (Ellis 1989: 202)

REBT's theory of personality stresses the equal importance of biology, sociality and psychology. The defining characteristic is how people make choices as conscious beings who have thoughts of which they are at times unaware. Ellis insists, however, that the self is not constituted by a 'reified unconscious' (Ellis 1989: 210)

The focus in REBT is on correcting irrational, self-defeating behaviours. The self has a capacity for 'magical thinking' and self-defeating 'irrational beliefs'. The self is constructed on irrational 'shoulds', 'oughts' and 'musts' that can be combated only through reason. These dogmatic clusters are a menace to the self and exemplify the self's potential for self-defeating behaviour. The self's capacity for dogmatism, overgeneralization, perfectionism, 'always' and 'never', shoulds-oughts-musts, excuses and rationalizations constitute the basis of dysfunction. By making use of the 'logico-empirical method of science to encourage people to surrender magic, absolutes, and damnation' (Ellis 1989: 233), REBT can free the self from the demands of an irrational and impossible striving for perfection. It seems the goal of REBT is to assist the self to achieve a more rational and homeostatic (balanced) existence with the demands of life.

In Britain, Dryden (1984) has been a prolific exponent of REBT with readers there being somewhat more familiar with his writings than with those of the American founder of REBT. All exponents of REBT advocate an 'active-directive' approach to therapy in the view that the self and personality are amenable to facilitated correction of self-defeating patterns.

Summary

In this chapter we have summarized some of the central tenets of cognitive psychology. We have focused especially on Susan Harter's work on the developmentally-evolving self-concept and have outlined some of the cognitive-developmental features of the self. We have also referred to REBT and the implications that theory has for selfhood and personality.

The final chapter examines several entirely different approaches to the self: those provided by the schools of humanistic, existential and transpersonal psychology. Whereas the cognitive-behavioural approaches align more strictly with western empirical science, humanistic, existential and transpersonal psychologies generally reflect on issues that move somewhat beyond the scientific frame, though not necessarily nor completely beyond the empirical grasp.

C H A P T E R   **8**

Humanistic, existential and transpersonal perspectives on the self

Within so called 'third force' psychology the self enjoys a renaissance of sorts. Recalling Chapter 1, after a brief culmination in the late nineteenth century, the self in psychology took a theoretical back seat. During the first half of the twentieth century behaviourism, experimental psychology and psychoanalysis more or less dominated the scene. During this brief but influential period, the self was nowhere to be seen, though, as we pointed out in Chapter 2, it was still at least implicitly there in the case of psychoanalysis. On rare occasions the early twentieth-century self did make an appearance acknowledged, for example in Mary Whiton Calkins (1908a, 1908b, 1908c, 1915) classic works on the self as well as Carl Jung's contributions, as pointed out in Chapter 6. However, the main thrust of early twentieth-century psychology clearly was focused on functional, behavioural and structural elements that generally precluded a central role for the self.

From within their respective corners of psychodynamic psychology, the Jungians, Adlerians and neo-Freudians did much to help reclaim the explicit self from theoretical obscurity. However, one might argue that influences from other corners of psychology gathered force and brought the self back into the foreground with even greater intensity. The sources of these influences are found in the *humanistic* and *existential* schools, the 'third force' in psychology (following behaviourism and psychoanalysis). Some neo-Freudians, and also the Adlerians, were part of this force, openly embracing humanistic and existential issues within the psychodynamic arenas. This chapter, however, will look at some of the 'purely' humanistic and existential contributions to the self, independent of the post-Freudians.

These include the *person-centred, existential* and *gestalt* schools, as well as the *transpersonal* school. In beginning with the latter, we realize that the transpersonal warrants a separate chapter, but space limitations compel us to include it amongst the humanistic and existential schools. It is a convenient placement, as many of the issues examined by the transpersonal school significantly overlap with the humanistic/existential. Moreover, some theorists have been strongly associated with both, for example Abraham Maslow and John Rowan are notable figures in humanistic and transpersonal psychology.

Transpersonal psychology and the self

Abraham Maslow recognized that the transpersonal school goes well beyond the humanistic and existential 'third force'. Perhaps this is why he sometimes refers to the transpersonal as the 'fourth force' in psychology. Specifically, transpersonal psychology is largely concerned with the ways in which *spirituality*, as distinct from any particular religious doctrine, affects the general psychology of human subjects. However, by invoking the 'spiritual', transpersonal psychology goes fundamentally beyond the personal psyche. Rowan makes this clear when he writes about 'the typical experience of contacting the transpersonal self': 'Sometimes it may be experienced as a total letting-go: this is the typical experience of contacting the divine, which may be known as energy, as nature, as god or goddess, as pure being' (1993: 3).

Unlike the humanistic schools, which draw on theorists who are atheist, agnostic or Theist, the transpersonalists generally do not find atheists represented within their sphere. As Rowan (1993: 220, original emphasis) elaborates, the transpersonal means 'being primarily interested in the human soul and divine spirit (*psyche* and *pneuma*)'. All transpersonal psychologists believe in something mystical, divine or numinous that goes beyond the self but is also integral to it. Perhaps this aspect is what renders the status of the transpersonal school as 'one of the outposts of psychology' (Rowan 1993: 13). If so, it is a significant one that has, perhaps in a roundabout way, influenced generations of counsellors and psychotherapists. We can safely make this claim, as the development of the school is in a sense 'multidisciplinary', with theorists from several differing schools within psychology contributing to the construction of this subdiscipline. For example, transpersonal psychology draws on theory and techniques from analytical psychology (for example Carl Jung and the post-Jungian James Hillman, see Chapter 2); the astrologer and philosopher Dane Rudhyar (1976); the founder of *psychosynthesis* Roberto Assagioli (1975), the psychoanalyst most famous for his studies on hallucinogenic drugs and altered states Stanislov Grof (1975); and the founder of *logotherapy* Victor Frankl (1963). We have already drawn attention to Abraham Maslow and John Rowan, and there are certainly many others who have contributed beyond this short list.

Amongst the empirical studies that have enhanced the status of the transpersonal school, allowing it to keep a foot within psychology as discipline, are those concerning the *peak experience*. Peak experiences (PE) have been described in detail by Maslow (1962) as phenomena that essentially go beyond words, that focus one's inspirations in an intense and profound manner. Examples of PE may include the experience of feeling very deeply moved, including 'mystical' feelings sparking reactions described as awe, grace, wonderment, extraordinary dazzle and a sense of time standing still. These spontaneous experiences can arise out of creative endeavours, hearing beautiful music, feeling struck by wondrous landscape, childbirth, hard won discoveries and so on. PEs often act as transformative incidents whereby the self itself can be deeply changed. In general terms, the more intense the PE, the more exceptional its effects. By definition these experiences are described as 'peak' insomuch as they go well beyond normal day-to-day events although they can certainly be rooted in them. PEs are, as noted by Rowan, 'key to the spiritual realms' (1993: 46).

Understanding the self in transpersonal psychology means understanding the spiritual self that goes beyond the material and social selves. For example, Rowan argues that the faculty of *intuition* is a primary factor in contacting what can be called the archetype of the transpersonal self, akin to Assagioli's (1975) 'superconscious' and 'higher self'. Specifically, Rowan sees intuition as a potential source of creative self-development, intuition as 'one's inner voice, one's inner sense, [it] can be a real guide to what direction to take in life choices' (1993: 14). In summarizing Rowan's views on intuition and its connection to the self we shall briefly summarize his six types of self, to which one presumably may become 'fixated' as a general modus of intuitive functioning:

1 *The child self*: in this phase, fantasy and reality are indiscriminate and the two can be confused.

2 *The magical self*: intuition is used to fuel one's retreat into a fantasy world. This generally acts as a defence mechanism in regard to loneliness or isolation.

3 *The role playing self*: the individual has disciplined intuition to the degree that it may be directed in the service of society. Here it is a skill that can be used productively such as in creative solutions brought to bear on a multitude of problems (scientific, social, artistic and so on).

4 *The autonomous self*: akin to the authentic, or towards the self-actualized self in humanistic psychology. One is able to express oneself as an individual without rehearsal, mimicry or in otherwise fake or concealed ways. The self expresses itself creatively and spontaneously.

5 *The surrendered self*: individual intuition is surrendered to a 'higher force' or some other factor. Rowan describes it as pure 'inspiration' and its source is well beyond the surface empiricism customary in psychology. One becomes a conduit for 'transpersonal energy'.

6 *The intuitive self*: here we quote Rowan (1993: 17), who describes this self as based on 'something like illumination or transcendence'. We assume that this level of achievement or being is relatively rare.

Humanistic psychology

The humanistic current in schools of counselling and psychotherapy emphasizes a view of self that is based on the here and now process of transparently becoming who we already are. This can occur when our basic material needs are met. Maslow (1943) argues that human beings live and function within a *hierarchy of needs*. The lower needs are essential to the sustenance of life and include food, shelter and intimacy; they move into 'higher' needs after being consistently fulfilled. The higher needs are what Monte describes as the 'classic "Goods" of the well lived life. Beauty, Truth, Justice, and many other capitalised virtues are the very core of the self-actualizer's existence' (1987: 502). These higher needs accord with the intrinsic need for humans to use *meaning* as a tool to self-actualize. At the higher echelon of needs, we find the possibility of peak experiences, which may facilitate self-actualization. Humanistic psychologists such as Rogers (1989) and May (1953) argue that the need to self-actualize is intrinsic.

If, as an ultimate purpose, we are to self-actualize, does this not suggest, as Kierkegaard certainly felt, that we have a 'real self' at our core? Rowan considers this idea in the context of deconstructionist and postmodern challenges. He asks, 'Is not the truth of the real self just the sort of truth which social constructionism is here to destroy?' (2000: 4). These debates extend somewhat beyond our scope here but nevertheless demand deeper contemplation.

Carl Rogers (1902–87), who founded the *person centred* school of psychotherapy, had surprisingly little to say about the explicit self, perhaps because of his preference for the term *person*. Nevertheless, there are some core implications evident in his work that can be extrapolated onto the self. First, the person-centred view shares with other humanistic schools the idea of field theory and therefore context, the self is best understood not as a thing, but as an active agent that is becoming in the here and now. Rogers (1989: 211) emphasizes 'the self as creator, the self as a free and self-determining being'. Rogers also emphasizes the human capacity for *empathy* as a central feature of the self. It can be revealed as an interpersonal force through what he calls *congruence* or authentic, open and genuine communication between empathetic actors. In emphasizing authenticity Rogers shares his wisdom based on experience:

> I have dealt with the maladjusted and troubled individuals, in the intimate personal relationship of psychotherapy, for more than a quarter of a century . . . if I were to search for the central core of difficulty in people as I have come to know them, it is that in the great majority of cases they despise themselves as worthless and unlovable . . . nearly all of these feelings are covered by some kind of a façade.
>
> (Rogers 1989: 211)

Dropping facades and becoming authentically who we are is central to the person-centred point of view. This is consonant with what Mearns refers to as *lace curtains*. Here he is drawing attention to a supposed characteristic of the British personality, and offers an example: 'One of the great British communal lace curtains is politeness . . . [this] protect[s] our Self from becoming visible to the other' (1998: 3). Using 'lace curtains' and 'safety screens' interchangeably, Mearns provides a reading of person-centred theory and the self that is dynamic (intrapersonal) as well as defensive in relation to others (interpersonal), constituting what he calls 'relational depth'. These dynamics refer to a 'configuration' of self whereby the self refers to 'a composite of its various configurations co-existing in a creative and self-protective conflict' (1998: 6). In utilizing an intrapsychic understanding of the self in person-centred work, Mearns cautions us:

> It may be tempting to go on to produce a detailed theory of Self by categorising different kinds of configurations and identifying common dynamics. Theories like that already exist. For example Transactional Analysis or object relations theory. However, that level of specification of theory is neither necessary nor helpful for person-centred working.
>
> (Mearns 1998: 7)

Mearns's viewpoint offers the general person-centred contention that imposing a reductive theoretical construction of self onto the person is not ultimately useful. Indeed, to do so would distract from the existential issues facing the whole person which such reductive theories ultimately fail to grasp. These issues are very similar to those outlined in gestalt theory, to which we will now turn our attention.

Gestalt therapy and the self

The gestalt therapy school developed out of the convergence of several important philosophical and psychological influences. It shares the name of a group of German perceptual psychologists whose detailed findings can be boiled down into the maxim *the whole is greater than the sum of its parts*. The gestalt academic psychologists conclude that wholes cannot be reductively broken-down into elements without compromising the integrity of the perceived configuration. This is essentially what the word *gestalt* (shape, figure) means, that is, the integrity of the whole.

The psychologist Kurt Lewin had a considerable impact on gestalt theory (referring now to the therapy rather than the distinct perceptual school of psychology). Lewin imported the notion of the *field* from physics into psychology as *field theory*. The field is the contextual totality of all co-existing parts, which are in constant flux and mutually interdependent. Gestalt theory takes field theory as central to its view of the self.

Fritz Perls (1839–1970) was a founding figure of the gestalt therapy school. Perls and his colleagues took the German gestalt psychologists' findings, that humans tend to make meaningful wholes through their perceptual fields, and went a step further by emphasizing this process as an impetus for making meaning. Pulling together meaning from the perceptual field brings together several important assumptions that Perls makes about the self.

First, the self is intrinsically linked to awareness – here and now awareness – so that reflection on past events or anticipation of the future are tied to a continuous and presently-embedded, perceiving subject. For this, and other reasons, the gestalt school emphasizes *phenomenology*.

Second, like Alfred Adler, Perls was deeply influenced by the philosophical writings of Smuts (1973) who, as pointed out in Chapter 5, emphasized *holism*. In a consistent vein, Perls also emphasized holism, arguing the need for integrity as a fundamental feature of human nature. For example, gestalt therapy attempts to foster integration and therefore the bringing together of dispersed, fractured or asundered psychic parts that the self requires to achieve homeostatic balance. In this regard, the self is a holistically functioning entity. To illustrate this point, perhaps crudely, a fractured wrist is seen as nevertheless contained holistically within the body – and one can similarly be whole on the macro level whilst experiencing psychic fractures on the micro level.

Third, the self in gestalt therapy is informed by humanistic ideas on one's unique potential. Kurt Goldstein's conception of *self-actualization* is evident in gestalt theory: people should become who they really are, in order to realize their core potentials, and strive for creative emergence. Such actualization occurs as part of the self's contextual interrelationships between the experiencing subject and the contexts in which he or she lives. Moreover, actualization is dependent on *contact*, which in gestalt theory refers to the interpersonal basis in which individuals become who they are. In this respect, Perls was also undoubtedly influenced by the nineteenth-century philosopher Kierkegaard's notion of *self-realization*. We note that Kierkegaard was far from being a humanist. Indeed, he is generally recognized as the founder of modern existentialism. However, Kierkegaard's notion of self-realization points to his deeply felt conviction that *true* selfhood resides at our core, a notion with which all humanistic psychologists concur. Clarkson and Mackewen provide a useful summary:

> Kierkegaard (1939) introduced the idea of self-realisation: he believed that it is the task of every person to become an entire person, by forming and renewing himself in the critical

decisions of life. Kierkegaard also emphasised personal responsibility, the truth of subjective experience and individuality.

(Clarkson and Mackewen 1993: 65)

There are some specific contributions to the theory of self that
have been made by the gestalt school. These ideas are enmeshed in
the conceptions laid out in field theory and the insistence on interpersonal relations. As Perls argues, there can be no self without the
other, which distinguishes both the I and the me. Perls also insists
that the more aware we are, the more aware we become of ourselves.
For example, he outlines how individuals become more self-aware
through *contact* and less self-aware when engaged in isolated introspection or less interaction with the world around them. The under-
pinning of self as contingent on interpersonality leads gestalt theorists
to emphasize self as *process* rather than self as thing. While the self
is posited as a process, for which the individual must accept responsibility as an autonomous being, such individuality, autonomy and
responsibility must nevertheless be contextualized. Clarkson and
Mackewen elaborate,

> whenever Perls emphasises individuality, commonality is in-
> evitably background, and when the need for connectedness is
> figure, the need for individuation is background. Commonality
> and individuality are poles that coexist, determine and define
> each other.

(Clarkson and Mackewen 1993: 63)

The self, in gestalt theory, undoubtedly draws from many other
philosophical influences, including Heidegger, Buber and Tillich. We
contend that the gestalt view of self bridges humanistic and existential factors as well as some neo-Freudian influences (for example
Sullivan). Indeed, Perls (1969) confirms his allegiance to existentialism in his book *Gestalt Therapy Verbatim*. In bridging such diverse
influences, the gestalt school registers its uniqueness in the third
force psychology movement. We will now look more specifically at
existential psychology's view of the self.

Existential psychology and the self

Entire treatises have been written on the self in existential philosophy, psychiatry and psychology. It would be difficult to recount

all the relevant issues around the self that such erudite works have already toiled to produce. We will, however, summarize the central issues that unite most who explore the self in an existential context.

Existentialism has distinct historical roots that go back a very long time, for example, Laotzu (d. 531 BC). As pointed out earlier, most credit the nineteenth-century philosopher Søren Kierkegaard (1813–55) as the most recent 'father' of existentialism in the west. Following Kierkegaard other notable figures that built existentialism include Martin Heidegger (1889–1976) and Jean-Paul Sartre (1905–80). The importation of philosophical existentialism into psychology, along with humanistic influences, is what constitutes the third force in psychology. In the United States of America, existentialism and humanistic psychology were both bridged and inaugurated by Rollo May (1909–94). In Britain R.D. Laing (1927–89) introduced existentialism to psychology (via psychiatry) through his analysis of schizophrenia. Also in Britain, Van Deurzen (1997) offers a contemporary reading of the self in existential psychology that draws together many diverse and theoretically challenging threads that run through the existential movement.

If we are to sufficiently understand something about the self as it is constructed in this school, then we need to ask what the general issues are that run thematically through the works of existential psychologists. We suggest that they are as follows: firstly, existentialism is concerned with *ontology* or the theoretical analysis of *Being*, which Heidegger linked with the German *Dasein* (roughly translated as 'human existence'). Human existence is an apparently simple but actually complex issue that concerns all existential psychologists, hence their emphasis on the nature of 'Being'. To 'be' means for them that the self becomes 'revealed or manifest' (Zimmerman 1981: xxviii). As self becomes revealed, it does not do so as a fixed thing or substance. Indeed, Heidegger's tripartite critique of the self (as subject, substance and self-consciousness) challenges the notion of a fixed, external self by placing selfhood within a temporal and finite frame that is subject to change. In this regard the importance of *authenticity* within the critique of self as substance becomes clear. Zimmerman summarizes Heidegger's position,

> Inauthentic self-understanding arises because we are unable to bear the truth about what it means to be human-that we are finite and mortal Being-in-the-world. In the face of our

mortality, we interpret ourselves as enduring substances. . . .
As authentic I disclose and accept my finitude and devote
myself to my own possibilities. I let myself be the finite openness which I already am.

(Zimmerman 1981: 30)

Rollo May, who initially was a pupil of Alfred Adler, argued that
at the core of the self one finds anxiety (angst). May insists that
anxiety is not always a negative phenomenon. Other existentialists
concur that existential anxiety exists due to our unique knowledge
of the inevitability of death. Our being in the world is a phenomenological interrelationship that is extinguished with death. Our
knowledge of death places us in a defensive relationship with the
world. May (1958) outlines three modes of being in the world: (1)
Umwelt or the world around us in a material sense, including our
biological basis and the objective environment; (2) *Mitwelt* or 'with
world', that is the interpersonal world of being with others and (3)
Eigenwelt or one's own world, the meaningful relationship that one
has with one's self. Van Deurzen (1997, 1998) adds a fourth dimension, the *Uberwelt*, which explicitly includes the spiritual dimension;
this, she points out, is generally implied in the works of Kierkegaard,
Nietzsche, Jaspers, Tillich and Buber.

R.D. Laing (1959) emphasizes the division between the real and
false selves in his classic book *The Divided Self*. The false self constitutes a defensive attempt to conform or comply with those around
one. This split between real and false selves arises out of early experiences with one's immediate family. The split is dynamically constel-
lated around 'ontological insecurity'. The danger with investing
in one's false self is that the inner or real self risks stagnation or
petrification. Underlying the self is an existential anxiety caused by
fear of imploding into nothingness, or a vacuum-based empty self:
a kind of death, or engulfment and loss of identity. Laing carefully
demonstrates how these issues come together in madness, using the
phenomenology of schizophrenia as an example.

Yalom (1981) contends that the self in existential psychology
is dynamic with unconscious elements constituting one's motives,
fears and anxieties. However, the dynamic existential self does
not necessarily concern itself with instinctual postulates as in psychoanalysis; rather it asserts the complexity of existence. Yalom
goes on to outline four ultimate concerns that dynamically occupy
the self. These are: (1) death; (2) freedom; (3) isolation and (4)
meaninglessness.

Summary and afterword

In this chapter we have briefly outlined issues pertaining to the self and personality in the transpersonal, humanistic and existential schools. Strong conceptual linkages exist across these schools, for example a concern with authenticity amongst the humanistic and existential schools, and with meaning and spirituality in the existential and transpersonal schools.

As has been evident throughout this volume, the self itself is a complex, multifarious, disparate and dynamic concept. Its vast terrain, what we may consider as personality theories, are just as complex. When considering specific aspects of the self, such as its autonomous vs. social, or its historical vs. biological components, it is easy to lose sight of this vastness. To borrow from the Gestalists, when focusing on important details of the self it is useful to keep in mind the perceptual *field*. The idea that these details exist within the field is considerably useful. It is within this context that the dialogue of hitherto competing theories of personality and psychotherapy may take place. Such a dialogue will consider questions relevant to all students, many of which are philosophical and part of the old and great 'human conversation'.

This leaves us with some final questions on the self and personality. What are the common threads that appear through the various perspectives? Are they relevant across time and space? How do individual selves reconcile within the contexts of culture and society, biology, psychology and spirituality? What future issues will emerge when looking critically at or 'problematizing' the self? Finally, is the self best approached henceforth through a detailed descriptive focus within traditional disciplinary boundaries (for example psychology, philosophy, sociology) or will an inter-multidisciplinary approach render more holistic data? What indeed is the personality of the self and can we ever fully know it?

Notes

Chapter 2

1 See, for example, Abraham's papers on 'The influence of oral erotism on character formation' (1925), 'Contributions to the theory of the anal character' (1923) and 'Character-formation on the genital level of libido' (1926) (Abraham 1966).

2 In Sigmund Freud's metapsychology, *drives* were associated with specific *bodily zones*; they had specific *aims*; and they were directed at specific targets or *objects*. Thus, in Kleinian metapsychology, 'object relations' have to do with intrapsychic relationships amongst mental representations of 'objects' – that is to say, *people*, one's self and others, the 'objects' of one's instinctual impulses or drives.

Chapter 3

3 Harlow (1960a, 1960b) demonstrated that young rhesus monkeys, provided with a choice between a terrycloth mother-surrogate and a wire mother-surrogate, preferred bodily contact with the terrycloth model despite the fact that the only food available came from the wire model. Food was *not* enough.

4 Later research has demonstrated many other infant behaviours that are reciprocal in nature and which predate the social smile.

Chapter 4

5 'Narcissistic' patients are those whose mode of relating to others is organized around protection and preservation of an exquisitely vulnerable 'self'

– a self whose vulnerability derives from the failure by early caregivers to attune themselves to the needs of their offspring. 'Borderline' patients are those who, despite their basically intact reality testing, tend to relate to others as all-good or all-bad; they lack a stable sense of self and of object constancy, have great difficulty managing normal ambivalence and are overdependent on external objects (people).

Chapter 6

6 Some citations of Jung's writings in this chapter follow the standard referencing (Jung 1953–1979): CW to *Collected Works* and *para.* to the numeric paragraph number as indicated in the Bollingen Series.

References

Abraham, K. (1966) *On Character and Libido Development: Six Essays*. New York: Basic Books.

Adler, A. (1927) *Understanding Human Nature*. New York: Greenberg.

Adler, A. (1956) In H.L. Ansbacher and R. Ansbacher (eds) *The Individual Psychology of Alfred Adler*. New York: Harper Torchbooks.

Adorno, T.W., Frenkel-Brunswik, E., Levinson, D.J. and Sanford, R.N. (1950) *The Authoritarian Personality*. New York: W.W. Norton.

Ainsworth, M.D. (1973) The development of infant-mother attachment, in B.M. Caldwell and H.N. Riccinti (eds) *Review of Child Development Research (Vol III)*. Chicago: University of Chicago Press.

Allport, G. (1937) *Personality: A Psychological Interpretation*. New York: Henry Holt.

Allport, G. (1955) *Becoming: Basic Considerations for a Psychology of Personality*. New Haven, CT: Yale University Press.

Andrews, B. (1998) Self-esteem, *The Psychologist*, 11(7): 339–42.

Ansbacher, H. (1999) Alfred Adler's concepts of community feeling and social interest and the relevance of community feeling for old age, in P. Prina, C. Shelley and C. Thompson (eds) *Adlerian Yearbook 1999*. London: ASIIP.

Assagioli, R. (1975) *Psychosynthesis: A Manual of Principles and Techniques*. London: Aquarian/Thorsons.

Barglow, R. (1994) *The Crisis of the Self in the Age of Information: Computers, Dolphins, and Dreams*. London: Routledge.

Beck, A.T. (1967) *Depression: Clinical, Experimental, and Theoretical Aspects*. New York: Hoeber.

Beck, A.T. and Weishaar, M.E. (1989) Cognitive therapy, in R.J. Corsini and D. Wedding (eds) *Current Psychotherapies*, 4th edn. Itasca, IL: F.E. Peacock Publishers.

Beebe, J. (ed.) (1989) *Aspects of the Masculine*. Princeton, NJ: Princeton University Press.

Beebe, J. (1998) Toward a Jungian analysis of character, in A. Casement (ed.) *Post-Jungians Today: Key Papers in Analytical Psychology*. London: Routledge.

Benvenuto, B. (1997) Once upon a time: The infant in Lacanian theory, in B. Burgoyne and M. Sullivan (eds) *The Klein-Lacan Dialogues*. London: Rebus Press.

Bick, E. (1964) Notes on infant observation in psychoanalytic training, *International Journal of Psycho-Analysis*, 45: 558–66.

Bick, E. (1968) The experience of the skin in early object relations, *International Journal of Psycho-Analysis*, 49: 484–6.

Bowlby, J. (1969) *Attachment and Loss, Volume I: Attachment*. New York: Basic Books.

Bowlby, J. (1973) *Attachment and Loss, Volume II: Separation – Anxiety and Anger*. New York: Basic Books.

Bowlby, J. (1980) *Attachment and Loss, Volume III: Loss – Sadness and Depression*. New York: Basic Books.

Bracken, B. (ed.) (1996) *Handbook of Self Concept: Developmental, Social, and Clinical Considerations*. New York: John Wiley and Sons.

Brod, H. (ed.) (1987) *The Making of Masculinities*. Boston, MA: Allen & Unwin.

Butler, J. (1990a) Gender trouble, feminist theory and psychoanalytic discourse, in L.J. Nicholson (ed.) *Feminism/Postmodernism*. London: Routledge.

Butler, J. (1990b) *Gender Trouble: Feminism and the Subversion of Identity*. London: Routledge.

Calkins, M.W. (1908a) Psychology as science of self: Is the self body or has it body? *Journal of Philosophy, Psychology and Scientific Methods*, 5: 12–30.

Calkins, M.W. (1908b) Psychology as science of self: The nature of the self, *Journal of Philosophy, Psychology and Scientific Methods*, 5: 64–8.

Calkins, M.W. (1908c) Psychology as science of self: The description of consciousness, *Journal of Philosophy, Psychology and Scientific Methods*, 5: 113–22.

Calkins, M.W. (1915) The self in scientific psychology, *American Journal of Psychology*, 26: 495–524.

Chodorow, N. (1994) *Femininities, Masculinities, Sexualities*. London: Free Association Books.

Clarkson, P. and Mackewen, J. (1993) *Fritz Perls*. London: Sage.

Cohler, B.J. and Galatzer-Levy, R.M. (1992) Psychoanalysis, psychology and the self, in J.W. Barron, M.N. Eagle and D.L. Wolitzky (eds) *Interface of psychoanalysis and psychology*. Washington, DC: American Psychological Association.

Connell, R.W. (1995) *Masculinities*. Cambridge: Polity Press.

Cooley, C.H. ([1902]1922) *Human Nature and the Social Order*. New York: Scribner.

Corsini, R.J. (1981) *Handbook of Innovative Psychotherapies*. New York: John Wiley.

Crisp, R. (1995) Character, in T. Honderich (ed.) *The Oxford Companion to Philosophy*. Oxford: Oxford University Press.

Damon, W. and Hart, D. (1988) *Self-understanding in Childhood and Adolescence*. New York: Cambridge University Press.

Danziger, K. (1997) Historical formation of selves, in R.D. Ashmore and L. Jussim (eds) *Self and Identity: Fundamental Issues*. Oxford: Oxford University Press.

Dreyfus, H.L. and Rabinow, P. (1982) *Michel Foucault: Beyond Structuralism and Hermeneutics*. London: Harvester Wheatsheaf.

Dryden, W. (1984) *Rational-Emotive Therapy: Fundamentals and Innovations*. Beckenham: Croom-Helm.

Ehrenwald, J. (ed.) (1991) *The History of Psychotherapy*. London: Jason Aronson Inc.

Ellenberger, H.F. (1970) *The Discovery of the Unconscious: The History and Evolution of Dynamic Psychiatry*. London: Penguin Press.

Ellis, A. (1980) Rational-emotive therapy and cognitive behaviour therapy: similarities and differences, *Cognitive Therapy and Research*, 4: 325–40.

Ellis, A. (1989) Rational-Emotive Therapy, in R.J. Corsini and D. Wedding (eds) *Current Psychotherapies*, 4th edn. Itasca, IL: F.E. Peacock Publishers.

Emde, R.N. (1983) The pre-representational self and its affective core, *Psychoanalytic Study of the Child*, 38: 165–92.

Emde, R.N. (1988) Development terminable and interminable: II. Recent psychoanalytic theory and therapeutic considerations, *International Journal of Psycho-Analysis*, 69: 283–96.

Emde, R.N. (1999) Moving ahead: Integrating influences of affective processes for development and for psychoanalysis, *International Journal of Psycho-Analysis*, 80(2): 317–39.

Erikson, E.H. ([1950]1963) *Childhood and Society*. New York: Norton.

Erikson, E.H. (1968) *Identity: Youth and Crisis*. New York: Norton.

Erikson, E.H. (1982) *The Life Cycle Completed: A Review*. New York: Norton.

Evans, B.F. (1996) *Harry Stack Sullivan: Interpersonal Theory and Psychotherapy*. London: Routledge.

Fairbairn, W.R.D. (1941) A revised psychopathology of the psychoses and psychoneuroses, *International Journal of Psycho-Analysis*, 22: 250–79.

Fairbairn, W.R.D. (1963) Synopsis of an object-relations theory of the personality, *International Journal of Psycho-Analysis*, 44: 224–5.

Finke, L. (1997) Knowledge as bait: feminism, voice and the pedagogical unconscious, in S. Todd (ed.) *Learning Desire: Perspectives on Pedagogy, Culture and The Unsaid*. London: Routledge.

Fordham, M. (1958) *The Objective Psyche*. London: Routledge and Kegan Paul.

Fordham, M. (1985) *Explorations into the Self*. London: Karnac Books.

Foucault, M. (1965) *Madness and Civilisation: A History of Insanity in the Age of Reason*. New York: Random House. [Abridged translation of *Folie et Déraison*, 1961.]

Frankl, V. (1963) *Man's Search for Meaning: An Introduction to Logotherapy*. New York: Pocket Books.

Freud, A. ([1936]1966) *The Ego and the Mechanisms of Defence*. London: Hogarth.

Freud, A. (1965) *Normality and Pathology in Childhood: Assessments of Development*. New York: International Universities Press.

Freud, S. ([1905]1953) Three essays on the theory of sexuality, in J. Strachey (ed.) *The Standard Edition of the Complete Psychological Works of Sigmund Freud*, vol. 7. London: Hogarth, pp. 125–243.

Freud, S. ([1923]1961) The ego and the id, in J. Strachey (ed.) *The Standard Edition of the Complete Psychological Works of Sigmund Freud*, vol. 19. London: Hogarth.

Fromm, E. (1998) *The Essential Fromm: Life between Having and Being*. New York: Continuum.

Geerardyn, F. (1997) The unconscious from a Lacanian point of view, in B. Burgoyne and M. Sullivan (eds) *The Klein-Lacan Dialogues*. London: Rebus Press.

Gergen, K.J. (1991) *The Saturated Self: Dilemmas of Identity in Contemporary Life*. New York: Basic Books.

Grof, S. (1975) *Realms of the Human Unconscious*. New York: Viking Press.

Grotstein, J.S. (1999) The alter ego and déjà vu phenomena: notes and reflections, in J. Rowan and M. Cooper (eds) *The Plural Self: Multiplicity in Everyday Life*. London: Sage.

Handlbauer, B. (1998) *The Freud–Adler Controversey*. Oxford: Oneworld.

Harlow, H.F. (1960a) Primary affectional patterns in primates, *American Journal of Orthopsychiatry*, 30: 676–84.

Harlow, H.F. (1960b) Affectional behaviour in the infant monkey, in M.A.B. Brazier (ed.) *Central Nervous System and Behavior*. New York: Josiah Macey Jr Foundation.

Harter, S. (1990) Developmental differences in the nature of self-representations: implications for the understanding, assessment and treatment of maladaptive behaviour, *Cognitive Therapy and Research*, 14(2): 113–42.

Harter, S. (1996) Historical roots of contemporary issues involving self-concept, in B. Bracken (ed.) *Handbook of Self Concept: Developmental, Social, and Clinical Considerations*. New York: John Wiley and Sons.

Hartmann, H. (1950a) Comments on the psychoanalytic theory of the ego, *Psychoanalytic Study of the Child*, 5: 74–96.

Hartmann, H. (1950b) Psychoanalysis and developmental psychology, *Psychoanalytic Study of the Child*, 5: 7–17.

Hartmann, H., Kris, E. and Loewenstein, R. (1947) Comments on the formation of psychic structure, *Psychoanalytic Study of the Child*, 2: 11–38.

Heine, S.J., Lehman, D., Markus, H.R. and Kitayama, S. (1999) Is there a universal need for positive self-regard? *Psychological Review*, 106: 766–94.

Hillman, J. (1983) *Archetypal Psychology*. Dallas, TX: Spring Publications.

Hillman, J. (1999) *The Force of Character: And the Lasting Life*. Toronto: Random House of Canada.

Hinshelwood, R.D. (1996) Convergencies with psychoanalysis, in I. Parker and R. Spears (eds) *Psychology and Society*. London: Pluto Press.

Hoffman, E. (1994) *The Drive for Self: Alfred Adler and the Founding of Individual Psychology*. New York: Addison-Wesley Co.

Horney, K. (1937) *The Neurotic Personality of Our Time*. New York: W.W. Norton & Co.

Jacoby, R. (1975) *Social Amnesia: A Critique of Conformist Psychology from Adler to Laing*. Boston: Beacon Press.

James, W. (1890) *The Principles of Psychology*. London: Harvard University Press.

Jung, C.G. (1953–1979) *The Collected Works of Carl Gustav Jung*, Vols 1–20. Princeton, NJ: Princeton University Press.

Jung, C.G. (1961) *Memories, Dreams, Reflections*. New York: Vintage Books.

Jung, C.G. (1968) *Analytical Psychology: Its Theory and Practice*. New York: Vintage Books.

Kant, I. ([1781]1965) *Critique of Pure Reason*. New York: St Martin's Press.

Kaplan, H.I. and Sadock, B.J. (1991) *Synopsis of Psychiatry: Behavioural Sciences, Clinical Psychiatry*, sixth edn. Baltimore, MD: Williams & Wilkins.

Kernberg, O.F. (1976) *Object Relations Theory and Clinical Psychoanalysis*. New York: Aronson.

Kernberg, O.F. (1982) Self, ego, affects and drives, *Journal of the American Psychoanalytic Association*, 30: 893–917.

Kernberg, O.F. (1995) Psychoanalytic object relations theories, in B.E. Moore and B.D. Fine (eds) *Psychoanalysis: The Major Concepts*. New Haven: Yale University Press, pp. 450–62.

Kihlstrom, J.F. (1992) The cognitive unconscious, in T. Nelson (ed.) *Metacognition: Core Readings*. Boston, MA: Allyn and Bacon.

Kimura, D. (1999) *Sex and Cognition*. Cambridge, MA: MIT Press.

Klein, J.T. (1990) *Interdisciplinarity. History, Theory and Practice*. Detroit, MI: Wayne State University Press.

Klein, M. ([1959]1975) Our adult world and its roots in infancy, in M. Klein, *Envy and Gratitude and Other Works 1946–1963*. London: Hogarth, pp. 247–63.

Kohut, H. (1971) *The Analysis of the Self: A Systematic Approach to the Psychoanalytic Treatment of Narcissistic Personality Disorders*. New York: International Universities Press.

Kohut, H. (1977) *The Restoration of the Self*. New York: International Universities Press.

Kohut, H. (1984) *How does analysis cure?* posthumously edited by A. Goldberg and P. Stepansky. Chicago: University of Chicago Press.

Kulkarni, C. (1997) *Lesbians and Lesbianisms: A Post Jungian Perspective*. London: Routledge.

Kulkarni, C. (1998) Radicalizing Jungian theory, in C. Shelley (ed.) *Contemporary Perspectives on Psychotherapy and Homosexualities*. London: Free Association Books.

Kurzweil, E. (1995) *Freudians and Feminists*. Oxford: Westview Press.

Laing, R.D. (1959) *The Divided Self*. Baltimore, MD: Penguin Books.

Lasch, C. (1979) *The Culture of Narcissism*. New York: W.W. Norton.

Lasch, C. (1984) *The Minimal Self*. New York: W.W. Norton.

Lather, P. (1991) *Getting Smart: Feminist Research and Pedagogy With/in the Postmodern*. London: Routledge.

Laurent, E. (1997) Rethinking Kleinian interpretation: What difference does it make? in B. Burgoyne and M. Sullivan (eds) *The Klein-Lacan Dialogues.* London: Rebus Press.

Linden, G.W. (1997) Adler and organ music, in P. Prina, C. Shelley and C. Thompson (eds) *Adlerian Yearbook 1997.* London: ASIIP.

McAdams, D. (1997) The case for unity in the (post)modern self, in R.D. Asmore and L. Jussim (eds) *Self and Identity: Fundamental Issues.* Oxford: Oxford University Press.

MacCary, W.T. (1998) *Hamlet: A Guide to the Play.* London: Greenwood Press.

McGuire, W. (ed.) (1974) *The Freud/Jung Letters: The Correspondence Between Sigmund Freud and C.G. Jung.* London: Penguin Books.

McHoul, A. and Grace, W. (1993) *A Foucault Primer: Discourse, Power and the Subject.* New York: New York Universities Press.

Mahler, M.S. (1968) *On Human Symbiosis and the Vicissitudes of Individuation, Volume I: Infantile Psychosis.* New York: International Universities Press.

Mahler, M.S., Pine, F. and Bergman, A. (1975) *The Psychological Birth of the Human Infant: Symbiosis and Individuation.* London: Hutchinson & Co.

Mahoney, M.J. (1990) Representations of self in cognitive psychotherapies, *Cognitive Therapy and Research*, 14(2): 229–40.

Markus, H. (1980) The self in thought and memory, in D.M. Wegner and R.R. Vallacher (eds) *The Self in Social Psychology.* New York: Oxford University Press.

Maslow, A. (1943) A theory of human motivation, *Psychological Review*, 50: 370–96.

Maslow, A. (1962) *Toward a Psychology of Being.* New York: Van Nostrand.

May, R. (1953) *Man's Search for Himself.* New York: Norton.

May, R. (1958) The origins and significance of the existential movement in psychology, in R. May, E. Angel and H.F. Ellenberger (eds) *Existence: A New Dimension in Psychiatry and Psychology.* New York: Basic Books.

Mead, G.H. (1934) *Mind, Self and Society.* Chicago, IL: University of Chicago Press.

Mearns, D. (1998) Working at relational depth: Person-centred intrapsychic family therapy. Paper presented to the joint conference of the British Association for Counselling and the European Association for Counselling, Southampton, England, 18 September.

Micale, M.S. (1993) *Beyond the Unconscious: Essays of Henri F. Ellenberger in the History of Psychiatry.* Princeton, NJ: Princeton University Press.

Modell, A.H. (1985) Object relations theory, in A. Rothstein (ed.) *Models of the Mind: Their Relationship to Clinical Work.* New York: International Universities Press, pp. 85–100.

Monte, C.F. (1987) *Beneath the Mask: An Introduction to Theories of Personality.* London: Holt, Rinehart & Winston.

Moore, B.E. and Fine, B.D. (eds) (1990) *Psychoanalytic Terms and Concepts.* New Haven: Yale University Press.

Murray, H. (1938) *Explorations in Personality.* New York: Oxford University Press.

Nietzsche, F. ([1886]1961) *Thus Spoke Zarathustra*. Harmondsworth: Penguin.

Paris, B.J. (1994) *Karen Horney: A Psychoanalyst's Search for Self-understanding*. London: Yale University Press.

Perls, F. (1969) *Gestalt Therapy Verbatim*. Moab, UT: Real People Press.

Pine, F. (1988) The four psychologies of psychoanalysis and their place in clinical work, *Journal of the American Psychoanalytic Association*, 36: 571–96.

Pine, F. (1990) *Drive, Ego, Object and Self: A Synthesis for Clinical Work*. New York: Basic Books.

Prince, M. (1906) *Dissociation of a Personality*. New York: Longmans, Green and Company.

Raoul, V. (1994) *Distinctly Narcissistic*. Toronto, ON: University of Toronto Press.

Reich, W. ([1928]1950) On character analysis, in R. Fliess (ed.) *The Psychoanalytic Reader*. London: Hogarth, pp. 106–23.

Rogers, C. (1989) Letter to Rollo May, in H. Kirschenbaum and V.L. Henderson (eds) *Carl Rogers: Dialogues*. London: Constable.

Ross, C.A. (1999) Subpersonalities and multiple personalities: A dissociative continuum? in J. Rowan and M. Cooper (eds) *The Plural Self: Multiplicity in Everyday Life*. London: Sage.

Rowan, J. (1993) *The Transpersonal: Psychotherapy and Counselling*. London: Routledge.

Rowan, J. (2000) Humanistic psychology and the social construction of reality, *Psychotherapy Section Newsletter*, British Psychological Society, Number 29, December: 1–8.

Rudhyar, D. (1976) *Astrology and the Modern Psyche*. Reno, NV: CRCS Publications.

Ryle, A. (1990) *Cognitive Analytic Therapy: Active Participation in Change*. Chichester: John Wiley.

Samuels, A. (1985) *Jung and the Post-Jungians*. London: Routledge and Kegan Paul.

Samuels, A. (1989) *The Plural Psyche: Personality, Morality and the Father*. London: Routledge.

Samuels, A. (1998) Will the post-Jungians survive? in A. Casement (ed.) *Post-Jungians Today: Key Papers in Contemporary Analytical Psychology*. London: Routledge.

Sandler, J., Holder, A., Dare, C. and Dreher, A.U. (1997) *Freud's Models of the Mind: An Introduction*. Madison, CT: International Universities Press.

Smuts, J.C. (1973) *Holism and Evolution*. London: Macmillan (first published 1925).

Spitz, R.A. (1957) *No and Yes: On the Genesis of Human Communication*. New York: International Universities Press.

Spitz, R.A. (1965) *The First Year of Life: A Psychoanalytic Study of Normal and Deviant Development of Object Relations*. New York: International Universities Press.

Stein, H. (1991) Adler and Socrates: similarities and differences, *Individual Psychology*, 47: 241–6.

Stern, D.N. (1985) *The Interpersonal World of the Infant: A View from Psycho-analysis and Developmental Psychology*. New York: Basic Books.

Sternberg, R.J. (1999) *Cognitive Psychology*, 2nd edn. New York: Harcourt Brace College Publishers.

Storr, A. (1983) Introduction, in A. Storr (ed.) *The Essential Jung*. Princeton, NJ: Princeton University Press.

Sullivan, H.S. (1950) The illusion of personal individuality, *Psychiatry*, 13: 317–32.

Swann, W.B. Jr (1996) *Self-Traps: The Elusive Quest for Higher Self-Esteem*. New York: W.H. Freeman.

Tacey, D.J. (1997) *Remaking Men: Jung, Spirituality and Social Change*. London: Routledge.

Thomas, K. (1996) The defensive self: A psychodynamic perspective, in R. Stevens (ed.) *Understanding the Self*. London: Sage.

Tolman, C.W. (1994) *Psychology, Society, and Subjectivity: An Introduction to German Critical Psychology*. London: Routledge.

Tong, R. (1989) *Feminist Thought: A Comprehensive Introduction*. London: Westview Press.

Tu, W. (1985) *Confucian Thought: Selfhood as Creative Transformation*. Albany, NY: State University of New York Press.

Vaihinger, H. ([1925]1965) *The Philosophy of 'as if'*. London: Routledge and Kegan Paul.

Vaillant, G.E. (1977) *Adaptation to Life*. Boston: Little, Brown.

Van Deurzen, E. (1997) *Everyday Mysteries*. London: Routledge.

Van Deurzen, E. (1998) *Paradox and Passion: An Existential Approach to Therapy and Counselling*. London: John Wiley and Sons.

Velten, E. (1998) Acceptance and construction: Rational emotive behaviour therapy and homosexuality, in C. Shelley (ed.) *Contemporary Perspectives on Psychotherapy and Homosexualities*. London: Free Association Books.

Wolfenstein, E.V. (1993) *Psychoanalytic Marxism: Groundwork*. London: Free Association Books.

Woolhouse, R. (1995) Locke, in T. Honderich (ed.) *The Oxford Companion to Philosophy*. Oxford: Oxford University Press.

Yalom, I. (1981) *Existential Psychotherapy*. New York: Basic Books.

Young-Eisendrath, P. (1998) Contrasexuality and the dialectic of desire, in A. Casement (ed.) *Post-Jungians Today: Key Papers in Contemporary Analytical Psychology*. London: Routledge.

Zimmerman, M.E. (1981) *Eclipse of the Self: The Development of Heidegger's Concept of Authenticity*. London: Ohio University Press.

Index